The Wickedness, Humiliation, Restoration and Reformation of Manasseh
by C. Matthew McMahon

Copyright Information

The Wickedness, Humiliation, Restoration and Reformation of Manasseh by C. Matthew McMahon
Edited by Therese B. McMahon

Copyright ©2019 by Puritan Publications and A Puritan's Mind®

Some language and grammar has been updated from any original manuscripts. Any change in wording or punctuation has not changed the intent or meaning of the original author(s) and has been made to aid the modern reader.

Published by Puritan Publications
A Ministry of A Puritan's Mind® in Crossville, TN.
www.apuritansmind.com
www.puritanpublications.com

All rights reserved. No part of this publication may be reproduced, stored in a retrieval system or transmitted in any form by any means, electronic, mechanical, photocopy, recording or otherwise, without the prior permission of the publisher, except as provided by USA copyright law.

This Print Edition, 2019
Electronic Edition, 2019

Manufactured in the United States of America

ISBN: 978-1-62663-323-0
eISBN: 978-1-62663-322-3

Table of Contents

Only Through Christ 4

Chapter 1: Manasseh's Wickedness 13

Chapter 2: Manasseh's Wickedness Part 2 59

Chapter 3: Manasseh's Humiliation and Restoration 89

Chapter 4: Manasseh's Reformation 117

Study Questions 145

Other Helpful Books by Puritan Publications 153

Only Through Christ
by C. Matthew McMahon, Ph.D.

The Puritan, Alexander Peden (1626-1686), once said, "Grace is young glory."[1] I agree. If believers are going to have a biblical view of grace, they ought therefore to use the term as the Bible uses it, not generally, but specifically, and in view of the glory which awaits the saint. God is pursuing his glory[2] and reflects that glory by grace to those who are believers in Jesus Christ. Grace becomes glory in all its wonder when the believer first enters heaven and takes their first breath. But where does that wonder of glory start? It starts here, on earth, under special circumstances, through *grace* – the unmerited favor of God to a fallen sinner.

Where is this *grace* found? The Bible never speaks of the grace of Jesus Christ being in *things* but always speaks of grace being *in Christ*. Grace, in and of itself, is not found in temples, altars, mercy seats, candlesticks, or bloody goats and lambs. Ephesians 1:3-6

---

[1] Thomas, I.D.E., *A Puritan Golden Treasury* (Carlisle: Banner of Truth Trust, 1989), 130.
[2] "For mine own sake, even for mine own sake, will I do it: for how should my name be polluted? and I will not give my glory unto another," (Isa. 48:11).

says, "Blessed be the God and Father of our Lord Jesus Christ, who hath blessed us with all spiritual blessings in heavenly places *in Christ*. According as he hath chosen us *in him* before the foundation of the world, that we should be holy and without blame before him in love: Having predestinated us unto the adoption of children *by Jesus Christ* to himself, according to the good pleasure of his will, To the praise of the glory of his grace, *wherein* he hath made us accepted *in the beloved*." Grace is "in Christ," "in him," and "in the Beloved" and only there is anyone accepted by God to receive grace. The Apostle Paul's conception of unmerited favor on a sinner is always *in Christ* as he clearly understood and expounded the Old Testament notion of a substitutionary atonement, and *never* outside of Christ. Looking through the rest of the epistle to the Ephesians one can see a variety of times that Paul uses this type of language. Whether there be 5, 10, or 100 spiritual blessings, there is no other *blessing* of salvation given but *in Christ alone*.

    The Greek construction of the phrase "every spiritual blessing" should better be translated "the entirety, *or all*, spiritual blessing," πάσῃ εὐλογίᾳ πνευματικῇ ἐν τοῖς ἐπουρανίοις ἐν χριστῷ, (Eph. 1:3).

Christians are blessed with the *whole* blessing of salvation *in Christ, all of it, lacking nothing*. It is not just the blessings themselves which Christians are blessed with, but the *entirety* of the spiritual blessing in Christ that they own, and they are sealed by the Spirit. After they have received this blessing, they then see its fruit in their lives.[3] Here one sees the immediate contrast between those who receive blessings in Christ and *those who do not*.[4] Those *in* Christ receive *grace*; those outside of Christ do not. Those outside of Christ have *no* spiritual blessings unless they have the *one complete spiritual blessing* in Christ which is given at regeneration through the Spirit.[5]

It is no coincidence that Ephesians 1:7ff shows that those who are in Christ receive "redemption," "forgiveness," and "an inheritance" to the "praise of His glory." Why is this so? Paul says that it is because of "His good pleasure which He purposed in Himself," and "the purpose of Him who works all things according to the

---

[3] "But the fruit of the Spirit is love, joy, peace, longsuffering, gentleness, goodness, faith, Meekness, temperance: against such there is no law. And they that are Christ's have crucified the flesh with the affections and lusts. If we live in the Spirit, let us also walk in the Spirit," (Gal. 5:22-25).
[4] See Galatians 5:19-21.
[5] "...by the washing of regeneration, and renewing of the Holy Ghost," (Titus 3:5).

counsel of His will." God's intention is to give the elect *grace in Christ* according to the eternal counsel and pleasure of his will. Romans 8:32 says, "He who did not spare His own Son, but delivered Him up for us all, how shall He not with Him also freely give us all things?" What are "all things?" The "all things" can be seen in Romans 8:29-30, "predestination," "calling," "justification," "glorification." All of these are "things" regenerated people receive in Christ. But God does not bless them with things merely "in and of themselves." He blesses them *by Christ, with Christ* and *in Christ.* All those "things given" pertain to his unbounded and infinite grace in the Lord Jesus! Paul even asserts in Romans 8:39 that *nothing* can separate Christ's people from the "love of God," which is, "*in* Christ Jesus." The blessing of grace is not in *things*, but rather, it is *solely* in Christ. Famous people who are interviewed at special galas often refer to the circumstances of making lots of money in their career, or having lots of material things, as being "blessed." "I'm so blessed," they say, that such and such a thing happened. It is true that tomatoes, cars, houses, friends, dogs, and the like, are given to men as things which are good; and the goodness of God in bestowing those things should lead people to repentance. But when God merely gives good things to people, *this is not grace*. It is a purposeful providence for an intended end. But to what end?

All fruit from God's grace in the life of a believer is found in *Christ alone* and leads them to a repentant life before God. Grace is not *in* tomatoes, cars, houses, friends, dogs, and the like. *In Christ* believers receive a great number of things which flow from the grace they have received. This, in turn, as you, reader, will see with Manasseh, turns to humility or repentance before God. They receive faith in Christ (Acts 24:24; Galatians 3:26), redemption in Christ (Romans 3:24), life in Christ (Romans 6:11; 8:2), love in Christ (Romans 8:39; 1 Timothy 1:14), sanctification in Christ (1 Corinthians 1:2), hope in Christ (1 Corinthians 15:19), justification in Christ (Galatians 2:16), kindness in Christ (Ephesians 2:7), consolation in Christ (Philippians 2:1), perfection in Christ (Colossians 1:28), boldness in Christ (1 Timothy 3:13), grace itself in Christ (2 Timothy 2:1), salvation in Christ (2 Timothy 3:15), and peace in Christ (1 Peter 5:14). Even these spiritual "things" are never detached from the grace found *in Christ*. Without Christ, without God's one and only Anointed Savior, they would not have *these things*. The lost and the reprobate do not have *any* of these things. Even those who will one day be elect at some future point, do not have these things until God saves them at a particular time and applies the work of redemption to them through the power of the Spirit *in Christ*.[6] Only those in Christ obtain these various gracious gifts enacted on them as elected individuals; not by a doing of their own, not of works lest any should boast, but by the work of Christ applied to them in his life, death, resurrection, ascension and exalted intercession on behalf of his own people.

It does not matter if we study the life of Abraham, or David, or *Manasseh,* or Apollos, or the Apostle Paul. If someone is born again, if someone is going to heaven, if someone is converted, if someone is saved, if someone is reconciled to God, justified, sanctified and glorified, it is *wholly* on account of Jesus Christ and the grace he bestows on them *in applying his saving work*. God only accepts people, any person, *in the Beloved*. Acceptance before God is solely based on the merits and work of Jesus Christ, being accepted "in

---

[6] Yes, they may have these things *virtually* considered, but not actually applied until a specific point in time by the work of the holy Spirit on their soul.

Him." This applies to every saint from any age of the church; it applies to *anyone* who goes to heaven.[7]

In considering the deplorable beginnings of Manasseh's life and reign, and the outcome of his reform, it is important to note that Manasseh *cannot* be saved in any other manner but by faith in Jesus Christ. For Manasseh, though, his faith looked forward to God's Anointed Savior *coming*. His faith was set in dark shadows and a veil obscured the full effulgent glory of the Redeemer to his spiritual senses. But make no mistake, "unless a man is born again he *cannot* enter the kingdom of heaven," (John 3:5). No one goes to heaven without being born by the Spirit, including wicked Manasseh converted by special grace sent by the throne of Christ by his Spirit to a very undeserving sinner; and it is exceptionally easy to say, *Manasseh was utterly unworthy of any grace whatsoever.*

Why study the life of Manasseh and the application of Christ's grace to such a wicked and deplorable man? Aside from the thief on the cross, I believe Manasseh is the "other" near deathbed convert to Christ that we find in the bible comparatively

---

[7] John 3:1-10, see that Christ there says that being born again is an Old Testament concept Nicodemus should have understood.

speaking. Certainly, there are many people converted who were wretches in Scripture. There are people in Scripture that were converted, saved and indwelt by the Spirit, who still, in some way, lived their lives short of God's glory – even further than most would like to allow.[8] But I think that Manasseh ought to hold a special place to two kinds of people. The first is the sinner who thinks they have sins that are bigger than Christ is a Savior. They are timid to come to him, believing that God might not save such a lost person as they are. And the second are believers who wonder how their sinning after conversion affects their standing before God, robbing them of the full assurance of faith[9] they should have *in Christ*. Manasseh gives us the ability to see how God works in the life of one of the most wretched people who ever lived, and how a despicable heathen can be converted and changed by the abundant power of Jesus Christ through the *covenant of grace*. As wicked as Manasseh might have been, God still reached down from heaven to change him, save him, reconcile him, and begin reformation not only of his own life, but life in the

---

[8] See, for example, the deplorable, yet faithful, life of Samson.

[9] "Let us draw near with a true heart in full assurance of faith, having our hearts sprinkled from an evil conscience, and our bodies washed with pure water," (Heb. 10:22).

church; he was used to change other people after his own conversion. Consider this as you read through this little work, that God saved a wretch like Manasseh from sin and hell, as abominable as he was, and abundantly pardoned him through saving grace only found in Jesus Christ. Such a truth should give sinners hope, and also give Christians a reason to cultivate a greater amount of godly assurance as they walk through the journey of this life before the face of God.

In the grace of Christ,
C. Matthew McMahon, Ph.D., Th.D.
From My Study, January, 2019

Chapter 1: Manasseh's Wickedness

"Manasseh was twelve years old when he began to reign, and he reigned fifty and five years in Jerusalem: But did that which was evil in the sight of the LORD, like unto the abominations of the heathen, whom the LORD had cast out before the children of Israel. For he built again the high places which Hezekiah his father had broken down, and he reared up altars for Baalim, and made groves, and worshipped all the host of heaven, and served them. Also he built altars in the house of the LORD, whereof the LORD had said, In Jerusalem shall my name be for ever. And he built altars for all the host of heaven in the two courts of the house of the LORD. And he caused his children to pass through the fire in the valley of the son of Hinnom: also he observed times, and used enchantments, and used witchcraft, and dealt with a familiar spirit, and with wizards: he wrought much evil in the sight of the LORD, to provoke him to anger. And he set a carved image, the idol which he had made, in the house of God," (2 Chron. 33:1-7).

Chapter 1: Manasseh's Wickedness

The writer of Chronicles seems to be the same writer of the book of Ezra.[1] The last two verses of 2 Chronicles are in fact the first two verses of the book of Ezra. Chronicles comprises one book, which was divided into two in the Greek translation of the Old Testament; but it was not originally divided into two books in the Hebrew. Great attention is given through the whole course of the history to matters of sanctified concentration, and, to matters of worship.[2] To balance the political aspects of the historical narrative, the Chronicler spent a huge amount of time balancing that back into the light of ecclesiastical (or *church*) concerns of the theocracy.

Chronicles is divided into 4 sections. Sections 1 and 2 deal with 1st Chronicles, sections 3 and 4 deal with 2nd Chronicles. Our passage falls into section 4, the history of successive reigns of the kings specifically of Judah, around 697 BC. 2 Kings 21:1-9 reflects similar material.[3] In 2 Kings the same information in this primary passage is also there. The difference between the two lies in a couple of small changes, and one

---

[1] It could possibly be Ezra.
[2] Worship is to be rendered to God only, Exod. 20:3; Deut. 5:7; 6:13; Matt. 4:10; Luke 4:8; Acts 10:26; 14:15; Col. 2:18; Rev. 19:10; 22:8.
[3] The reader may want to take some time to read that section before moving on.

expansion. In 2 Kings, Manasseh's mother is mentioned. Hephzibah, which means "My delight is in her," (*cf.* Isa. 42:4). There is also the expansion of the message which God sent by the prophets to Manasseh and the people on account of their wickedness. This will be more applicable in chapter 3.

For our purposes, we will only deal with verses 1-7a. "Manasseh was twelve years old when he became king, and he reigned fifty-five years in Jerusalem." This was the longest reign of any king, and sadly, Manasseh had the most wicked reign. Is it not odd that the commentary of his life, reaches all the way back from the time he reigned? He was only 12, but Manasseh *did evil* in the eyes of the Lord even from that time. Surely, "The heart is deceitful above all things, and desperately wicked: who can know it?" (Jer. 17:9). And, "The wicked are estranged from the womb: they go astray as soon as they be born, speaking lies." (Psa. 58:3). At whatever age one would like to consider Manasseh, albeit he being 12, 20, 30, 40, or 50, Manasseh *was wicked.*

"But he did evil in the sight of the LORD, according to the abominations of the nations whom the LORD had cast out before the children of Israel." He forgot, it seems, any good heritage he would have received from Hezekiah his father. It calls into question at some level that Proverb, "Train up a child in the way he should go, And when he is old he will not depart from it," (Prov. 22:6). When he began reigning was he evil? It seems, Manasseh was already lost to the world at a young age. It does not matter whether one is young or old as one of Adam's progeny.[4] Old vs. young, still, there seemed to be a lack of training for this young man,[5] and even at the age of 12, being robbed of his father, or so he might have thought, he began his autonomous path toward utter destruction and ruin. This is not necessarily the fault of Hezekiah, for many godly fathers have done their very best with raising covenant children and yet, they turn out to be covenant breakers.[6] Heritage does not ensure grace. Grace is not in the blood. It

---

[4] "Wherefore, as by one man sin entered into the world, and death by sin; and so death passed upon all men, for that all have sinned," (Rom. 5:12).

[5] "Train up a child in the way he should go: and when he is old, he will not depart from it," (Prov. 22:6).

[6] "But now, O LORD, thou art our father; we are the clay, and thou our potter; and we all are the work of thy hand," (Isa. 64:8). Was not God the Father of his people, and yet, "Furthermore the LORD spake unto me, saying, I have seen this people, and, behold, it is a stiffnecked people," (Deut. 9:13). Was God a delinquent Father because the people were stiffnecked or wicked? "I have seen also in the prophets of Jerusalem an horrible thing: they commit adultery, and walk in lies: they strengthen also the hands of evildoers, that none doth return from his wickedness: they are all of them unto me as Sodom, and the inhabitants thereof as Gomorrah," (Jer. 23:14). This does not make God a poor Father.

cannot be transmitted simply as the Pharisees thought, as being a child of Abraham.[7]

This Manasseh was *evil* in God's sight. Everything God instructed kings to do or not do Manasseh responds with wickedness.

> "When you come into the land which the LORD your God is giving you, you shall not learn to follow the abominations of those nations. There shall not be found among you anyone who makes his son or his daughter pass through the fire, or one who practices witchcraft, or a soothsayer, or one who interprets omens, or a sorcerer, or one who conjures spells, or a medium, or a spiritist, or one who calls up the dead. For all who do these things are an abomination to the LORD, and because of these abominations the LORD your God drives them out from before you. You shall be blameless before the LORD your God. For these nations which you will dispossess listened to soothsayers and diviners; but as for you, the LORD your God has not appointed such

---

[7] "And think not to say within yourselves, We have Abraham to our father: for I say unto you, that God is able of these stones to raise up children unto Abraham," (Matt. 3:9).

for you. The LORD your God will raise up for you a Prophet like me from your midst, from your brethren. Him you shall hear," (Deut. 18:9-15).

He did everything in opposition to the Law, everything in opposition to God's revealed will, and everything in opposition to worship and the Regulative Principle.[8] God *alone* determines the manner in which sinners approach him.[9] Manasseh determined what he thought would be acceptable gain for himself. Everything he did was in opposition to his earthly father as well as his heavenly Father.

Manasseh is known for destroying the godly reformation begun by his father Hezekiah. Think of it, everything opposite to goodness and truth he instituted in place of reformation. Everything in opposition to the prophets or ministers and their message.[10] Everything evil. What did he do – the text says that *all he did was evil.* Christ informs his disciples that they are to pray

---

[8] "Therefore shall ye lay up these my words in your heart and in your soul," (Deut. 11:18).
[9] "But in vain they do worship me, teaching for doctrines the commandments of men," (Matt. 15:9).
[10] "For this cause also thank we God without ceasing, because, when ye received the word of God which ye heard of us, ye received it not as the word of men, but as it is in truth, the word of God, which effectually worketh also in you that believe," (1 Thess. 2:13).

daily, "Deliver us from evil," (Matthew 6:13). The basic practice of the church is daily prayer for deliverance in spiritual opposition to everything contrary to the Word of God and holiness.[11] That which is *evil* is to be despised and cast off.[12] Manasseh only did *evil*.

Every derogatory Word associated with the revealed will of God in the Law is summed up by this Word *evil*.[13] But let us hear some of his specific evils. "For he rebuilt the high places which Hezekiah his father had broken down; he raised up altars for the Baals, and made wooden images; and he worshiped all the host of heaven and served them." He reversed the revival of religion and the reformation that had begun. That in and of itself is heinous; all that Hezekiah had done in settling godly worship and good Christian virtues before God, Manasseh overturned. Not only did he do *something* evil in God's sight, but he consciously *repealed the reformation*. He was overthrowing everything good to do everything evil.

Manasseh established High places. Ashteroth was a Canaanite deity associated with Baal worship, she

---

[11] "I do not ask Thee to take them out of the world, but to keep them from the evil *one*," (John 17:15).
[12] "Abhor that which is evil; cleave to that which is good," (Rom. 12:9).
[13] Rom. 14:1–23; 1 Cor. 8:7–13, 10:28–33; 1 Thess. 4:11-12, 5:22.

was a fertility goddess. "They forsook the LORD and served Baal and the Ashtoreths," (Judges 2:13). She was one of three goddesses of sex and war, and these three goddesses were known as *sacred prostitutes*, with temple prostitutes, in which the worshipper would have had relations as part of his worship. She would have been represented by a kind of wooden cult object set up in "high places" beside incense altars and stone pillars. Manasseh set those up. What was he thinking? To set those up would be to set up the prostitution that went along with it, to recruit for it.

Baal was the god of the thunderstorm, who personified the power of all nature; he was the son of Dagon, the fish god. Manasseh set up altars to sacrifice to the "lord", which is translated as *Baal* from the Canaanite word. He set up wooden images to Baal. This was blatant idolatry at its highest. To not only worship Baal, but to create and have fashioned images to Baal. Vocations for this would have to be made. Recruitment for this would have to occur. People would have been convinced by him to *do* evil.

Manasseh worshipped the host of heaven. The pantheon of gods was at his disposal. In the astrological cults of antiquity, it was believed in such paganism that celestial bodies were animated by spirits and in this way constituted a heavenly army that controlled destiny. They are particularly worshipped by the idolatrous Israelites during the times of the Assyrian and Babylonian periods. He would have had to gather around himself people who knew these things, or, train them; or recruit *and then* train them.

"He also built altars in the house of the LORD, of which the LORD had said, "In Jerusalem shall My name be forever." Like spitting in the face of God, Manasseh has altars built in the temple, so that in a singular location all types of worship could take place; a one stop shop. The Chronicler makes this a reference from Deut. 12:11, "then there will be the place where the LORD your God chooses to make His name abide. There you shall bring all that I command you: your burnt offerings, your sacrifices, your tithes, the heave offerings of your hand, and all your choice offerings which you vow to the LORD." He built altars in a sacred spot where only the worship of God should take place. He invaded God's sanctuary.

"And he built altars for all the host of heaven in the two courts of the house of the LORD." In the courts he erected idolatry simply because there was space; he built more altars for the pantheon of gods from the neighboring nations. There was the court,[14] the holy place[15] and the holy of holies.[16] In his mind all of this was good real-estate and he should use it all.

"Also he caused his sons to pass through the fire in the Valley of the Son of Hinnom; he practiced soothsaying, used witchcraft and sorcery, and consulted mediums and spiritists. He did much evil in the sight of the LORD, to provoke Him to anger." This is a reference to the Valley of the Son of Hinnom.[17] The idolatrous Jews here erected a statue of Molech made of brass. "And you shall not let any of your descendants pass through the fire to Molech, nor shall you profane the name of your God: I am the LORD," (Lev. 18:21). "He [Ahaz] burned incense in the Valley of the Son of Hinnom, and burned his children in the fire, according to the abominations of the nations whom the LORD had cast out before the children of Israel," (2 Chron. 28:3). Manasseh sacrificed his children, *infants*, in the fire. It could be possible that these children were born of temple prostitution. Regardless, some of the children that Manasseh passed

---

[14] 2 Chron. 29:16.
[15] 2 Chron. 5:11.
[16] 2 Chron. 3:10.
[17] 2 Kings 23:10; Jer. 7:31-32.

through the fire to Molech could have been kings (they were *his sons*). His heritage was burned alive in sacrifice to the devil, to false gods. Is this a horrible thought? Later, the Valley of the Son of Hinnom was deemed *Tophet*, meaning place of fire.[18] This Valley of the Son of Hinnom, or *Gehenna* in Greek is the Word Christ uses translated *hell*.[19]

Manasseh instituted soothsaying. This is foretelling events to produce or conjure up something concerning one's future. *Sooth* is an old English Word to signify *truth*. Instead of "in good truth," men were accustomed to say, "in good sooth." This is akin to *good luck,* a demonic kind of foretelling of the future where arrows were shot into the sky to see where the demons would push them, left or right, towards their mark to render a certain verdict based on an asked question about the future. Today, Christians are given over to this

---

[18] "For Tophet is ordained of old; yea, for the king it is prepared; he hath made it deep and large: the pile thereof is fire and much wood; the breath of the LORD, like a stream of brimstone, doth kindle it," (Isa. 30:33).

[19] "And fear not them which kill the body, but are not able to kill the soul: but rather fear him which is able to destroy both soul and body in hell," (Matt. 10:28).

practice when they wish people "good luck", or use terms like, "it was lucky that happened."[20]

Manasseh instituted witchcraft. Witchcraft deals with evil spirits and those claiming to have special supernatural power which manipulate circumstances. William Perkins said, "Witchcraft is a wicked art, serving for the working of wonders, by the assistance of the devil, so far forth as God shall in justice permit."[21] It is making a league with the devil. It is selling the soul in covenant to the devil. Manasseh consulted with the devil in these things. This was not an ignorant gesture. *He consulted with the devil.* This is why God says in Exodus 22:18, "Thou shalt not suffer a witch to live."

Manasseh instituted sorcery which dealt with charms and magic spells. It housed casting lots of divinations to foretell future arbitrary events. There is in this a superadded direction and assistance of the Devil. There is nothing of God in this. Sorcery indicates a diabolical art, which is fashioned by the help of the devil.

Manasseh instituted and allowed the practice of mediums. These were people who acted as a channel of

---

[20] For a full discourse on this topic, see Nathaniel Holmes work, *Demonology and Theology*, pages 69ff, (Crossville, TN: Puritan Publications, 2014).
[21] Perkins, William, *A Discourse on the Damned Art of Witchcraft*, (Coconut Creek, FL: Puritan Publications, 2012) 10.

communication between human beings and what they think is the spirit world. It also houses the art of Necromancy – one who supposedly speaks with the dead. This is called the Black Art, which is a divining by consultation with the devil appearing to the diviners in the shape of one formerly dead. For example, the witch of Endor raised up for Saul some shape of Samuel, some demon, some devil, imitating him.[22] This is forbidden, as given in Deuteronomy 18:11. "There shall not be found among thee a Necromancer," אֶל־הַמֵּתִים, *i.e.* one that seeks information from the dead.

    Manasseh also allowed spiritists, or those able to communicate with familiar spirits, such as the witch of Endor. The devil makes the witch his immediate instrument in divination, when he immediately informing the witches and diviners, enables them to tell many hidden things, speaking in them or by them. In this respect in part, the devil or his demons are called *familiar spirits*, and the diviner is called one that *has* a familiar spirit. Lev. 19:31, "you shall not regard them that work with spirits." Again, Lev. 20:6, "If any turn after

---

[22] "And Saul disguised himself, and put on other raiment, and he went, and two men with him, and they came to the woman by night: and he said, I pray thee, divine unto me by the familiar spirit, and bring me him up, whom I shall name unto thee," (1 Sam. 28:8).

such as work with spirits, to go a whoring after them, I will set my face against that person, and will cut him off from among his people." And, Deut. 18:11, "Let none be found among you, that consulteth with spirits." And it was said of the witch at Endor, "Behold, there is a woman that hath a familiar spirit at Endor," (1 Sam. 28:7). Familiar spirits are those imitating people who have died, like Samuel. Demons know much about them because they have followed them all their lives. They are *familiar* with them, and they communicate in their stead to deceive people thinking they are speaking with spirits. They think they are speaking with long departed Harry, where they are in fact speaking to some demon deceiving them.

The list of sins that Manasseh instituted is tiring – Manasseh did *much* evil. "He even set a carved image, the idol which he had made, in the house of God, (2 Chron. 33:1-7a)." Not only did he reverse the reformation Hezekiah had begun, but *established* the exact opposite of everything God commanded the people, and participated in its specific establishment in setting up an idol or carved graven image in God's house, which the text says, *he made*. He not only recruited, trained, and deceived the people, seduced them, but he had his very own hands involved in making something he thought was special.

All these things Manasseh did "...to provoke [God] to anger..." This is a negative Hebrew Word used exclusively of making God *angry*. Every time it is used, it concerns sin. God was vexed, filled with indignation and anger, in an absolute sense against Manasseh's sin. The Chronicler wanted the reader to understand that Manasseh pushed and pressed and prodded God along to *erupt a great anger*. Both Kings and Chronicles make the note that all this evil was so degenerate, verse 9 in both texts, that Manasseh did "more evil than the nations whom the LORD had destroyed before the children of Israel," (2 Kings 21:9). He not only rejected the light of God, but he did everything to destroy the light. He implemented *the darkness*.[23]

In defiling worship and leading the people astray, Manasseh provoked God more than any other fallen human being on the planet up until this point. He was worse than the other nations. He was worse than *wicked* nations in *darkness*.[24] The first miserable sinner

---

[23] "Wherefore their way shall be unto them as slippery ways in the darkness," (Jer. 23:12).
[24] "Who in times past suffered all nations to walk in their own ways," (Acts 14:16).

Chapter 1: Manasseh's Wickedness

is Adam that sent all of humanity plummeting into the abyss of hell in his fall. Later, there is Paul who says he is the chief among sinners in sinning against Christ and persecuting the Gospel by murder.[25] Manasseh has gained the reputation of being in the top three. And this is not only in his own sin, but in leading others to do the same. God so says, "Therefore thus says the LORD God of Israel: 'Behold, I am bringing such calamity upon Jerusalem and Judah, that whoever hears of it, both his ears will tingle,'" (2 Kings 21:12). This does not refer to just those going through it, rather, those who *hear* about it. Judgment will be so terrible and so bad that rumors of it will cause people to tremble and quake. And in all this, Manasseh was a terrible, wicked, evil man in league with the devil himself.

Provoking sins of this kind anger the Almighty God, whether it is one sin, or thousands.[26] Consider the nature of God and sin.[27] When one considers the nature

---

[25] "This is a faithful saying, and worthy of all acceptation, that Christ Jesus came into the world to save sinners; of whom I am chief," (1 Tim. 1:15).

[26] "Remember, do not forget how you provoked the LORD your God to wrath in the wilderness; from the day that you left the land of Egypt until you arrived at this place, you have been rebellious against the LORD," (Deut. 9:7).

[27] "The LORD tests the righteous and the wicked, And the one who loves violence His soul hates," (Psa. 11:5). Question 14 of the Westminster Shorter Catechism asks, "What is sin?" Answer: Sin is

of God, they study him by way of separate attributes, and separate actions. As the *1647 Westminster Confession of Faith* states, God is not made up of *parts* but is *one* spirit.[28] He is also not made up of separate passions. Believers cannot fathom God in this simple unified way. They must think about him consecutively, by comparing one bit of information about an attribute, with another. They have to think about holiness, and how it relates to justice. They think about how love relates to goodness. In contrast, God exists in constant delight within himself;[29] eternally blessed;[30] he thinks about himself in a single perfect, infinite, all-encompassing *thought*.[31]

How does God want Christians to think about him; and how are they to consider his dealings with sin?

---

any want of conformity unto, or transgression of, the law of God. (Lev. 5:17; James 4:17; 1 John 3:4).

[28] *1647 Westminster Confession of Faith* 2:1, "There is but one only living and true God, who is infinite in being and perfection, a most pure spirit, invisible, without body, parts, or passions..."

[29] "But let him that glorieth glory in this, that he understandeth and knoweth me, that I am the LORD which exercise lovingkindness, judgment, and righteousness, in the earth: for in these things I delight, saith the LORD," (Jer. 9:24).

[30] "God blessed for ever. Amen," (Rom. 9:5).

[31] Consider all the "I am" verses in which God communicates something of himself as the great I AM to his people. "I am El-Shaddai—'God Almighty,' (Genesis 17:1). "I Am Who I Am," (Exodus 3:14), *etc.*, (*cf.* Exodus 6:2, 15:26, 20:2, 22:27, 34:6; Leviticus 18:5; Psalm 46:10; Isaiah 28:16, 41:10, 42:8, 43:11-13, 46:9).

We read in Scripture, "For a fire is kindled in mine anger, and shall burn unto the lowest hell, and shall consume the earth with her increase, and set on fire the foundations of the mountains," (Deut. 32:22). Then consider, "God loveth a cheerful giver," (2 Cor. 9:7). In the passage of 2 Chronicles concerning Manasseh, it *seems* to infer (or is it eminently blatant) that Manasseh's sins "provoke him to anger...." But, when someone gives cheerfully God then responds in love; he loves that. All these seem like God has "responses" to human actions. How many trillions upon trillions of human actions does God respond to daily in this way? Does God change the way he feels and acts *every* nanosecond? How many of these changes are overlapped one upon another to trillions and trillion of times every second by billions of people? Men do something God hates and so God is provoked by that, like sticking him with a knife each time to see him twitch here and there? Then they do something good and he *changes* to respond to that. He does this billions of times every second? This would hardly make God *blessed* and *eternally content*. It would seem, men would frustrate him, and that, constantly. Yet, Scripture says, "For I am the LORD, I change not; therefore ye sons of Jacob are not consumed," (Mal. 3:6). This is odd, then. When men sin against God, he gets angry. When they please him, he becomes happy. Well, with billions of people alive today, God is switching back and forth *constantly*. With all the people, all the time all over the planet, every second of every day for all of history he is *ever changing*? Is God really *that* reactionary? "I the Lord do not change" but, it *seems* to say he gets angry and is *provoked*.

Passions, or affections, that describe God in Scripture, such as love, hatred, anger, jealousy, patience, and the like, are used to describe God's actions in human terms, so Christians can understand their relationship to God in the action more clearly. The Bible describes God in language *accommodated* to the human mind and its understanding; yet, those terms are used *figuratively*. They are speaking after the manner of men, so that men can understand their relationship to God. This concept is very important because it separates God from idols. It separates God *in the text* of *2 Chronicles* from idols. Idols can be prompted, prodded, persuaded and they can *change, so to speak*. Idols are certainly mute and have no intrinsic ability to do anything (they are made of wood or metal or other material substances). But the way life appears to occur when a person prays to an idol, all this is based solely on the person worshipping the idol and what they think or what they interpret providence to mean in light of their request to it, or in all actuality, to the devil.[32] When people pray to an idol, the devil is listening. What will be manipulated by the principalities and powers who are listening to the requests when people pray to idols? What will God allow them to do? Manasseh's idolatry is seen in his setting up of various departments of worship for various gods that respond to various needed blessings. This is why there is such a wide variety of evil in Manasseh's sins. He tried it all. He opened the door to everything possible for "spiritual direction," except of course, to hear and listen to the one true Living God.[33] So how is the phrase "God provoked" to be understood?

Consider a bon-fire in a field. A great bon fire, contained in the middle of a football field, burns there so hot and radiating that the closer one comes to it, the more they feel the heat. The further they walk away from it, the colder it gets. Does the fire actually get colder? (Do

---

[32] Demons hover around and on idolatry and idols. "They provoked him to jealousy with strange gods, with abominations provoked they him to anger. They sacrificed unto devils, not to God; to gods whom they knew not, to new gods that came newly up, whom your fathers feared not," (Deut. 32:16-17).

[33] "We trust in the living God, who is the Saviour of all men, specially of those that believe," (1 Tim. 4:10).

you see the use of the language I chose?) This is the way the person walking away from it perceives it. The closer they walk towards it the hotter it is. Does it actually "get" hotter? If they go too close to the fire, it will kill them. They cannot get *too close*. The fire is too intense. The California wild fires in 2018 that were raging across the state had fires of 1000's of degrees melt steel. To get merely *too close* to that is to be burned up; people had to *get away* from the fire. Their relationship with the fire was one which caused them to run from it, to move away from it, so that they would be safe. As one gets close to the fire, the fire becomes hotter, or so they perceive it this way. It is, in truth, hotter the closer the person walks to it. As one gets further away from the fire, the same fire is cooler. When one is out of range, the fire itself isn't even felt. Does the *fire* change? Or does the relationship of the person to the fire change? Considering the way the Chronicler wants the reader of this text to come away with an idea of what it means that *God is provoked* by sin or not; well, the closer one is to the fire, the hotter God feels to them; the further away from the fire, the cooler. The person's nearness to the fire, in his steps, determines if the fire feels hotter or cooler. The fire never changes. It rages on. The person, depending on *their position to the fire*, feels the fire's heat, or not.

In considering that crude illustration, God is not *reactionary*, where one second he is hot, and another second he is cold, depending on the actions of people. No, God is ever the same. As a matter of fact, "our God *is* a consuming fire," (Heb. 12:29). He neither waxes or wanes. He is ever the same, yesterday, today and forever.[34] God says of himself, "I the Lord change not."[35] But, people change in their mutability. Their relationship to God changes. Further the illustration in this way – two people experience the bon-fire. One is 50 feet away, and the other is 50 miles away. They meet up the next day. One says, *did you feel the heat of the fire?* The other replies, *I didn't even know there was a fire.* The relationship God has with sinners is much the same. Their act of sin, or not, determines the heat of the fire, or what is perceived they feel. Their relationship with God changes in this way. They walk closer to the fire, God is angry. Further away, he is happy. But this is all speaking

---

[34] "Jesus Christ the same yesterday, and today, and for ever," (Heb. 13:8).
[35] God is forever unchanging. Num. 23:19; 1 Sam. 15:29; Isa. 46:10; Mal. 3:6; Rom. 11:29; 2 Tim. 2:13; Heb. 6:18.

after the manner of men in biblical accommodation to the finite minds of men.

God has given the church his Word so that they have a temperature gage, and that gage has certain readings on it. How shall the Chronicler explain to his readers that God *hates sin?* That he is *utterly opposed* to it and is *provoked* by it? When they sin against God, God is angry. When they please God, God is happy. How shall he tell them this? This is speaking after the manner of men. This kind of language helps those who read the Bible know God's relationship to these things should never be considered as *indifferent.* There is a real provoking that Scripture exemplifies to the church that when people sin against God, God should be thought of as being provoked by it because *their* relationship to God changes; and they walk closer to the fire as a result.

In this, God is more provoked by idolatry than one might imagine. On a basic level idolatry is not only spiritual adultery from God's will revealed in scripture, but it is self-love.[36] Idolatry is to conceive or have something else in which one places their trust instead of, or besides, the one true God who has revealed himself in

---

[36] "Mortify therefore your members which are upon the earth; fornication, uncleanness, inordinate affection, evil concupiscence, and covetousness, which is idolatry," (Col. 3:5).

his Word. *The mind is a factory of idols*, Calvin said.[37] It is when a person says, *I will not do what God wants me to do, rather, I will do what I think to be best and what pleases me most for my benefit at this time*. They do something from what they have learned, or from their traditions, or even from what they think is simply best. It is all about *me, me, me*.

God's wrath[38] is provoked when his bride (the church) violates his rights as groom, as the husband, by following after other gods, other lovers,[39] committing idolatry which is spiritual adultery.[40] God is provoked in jealousy for his glory which he will not have tainted.[41] Jealousy is not an attribute of God, but an adapted expression of a change in relationship, centering on the absence of divine love.[42] "For they provoked him to anger with their high places, and moved him to jealousy

---

[37] Calvin, John, *Institutes of the Christian Religion*, 1.11.8.
[38] God is wrathful. Psa. 2:11; Prov. 16:6; Mal. 2:4-6; Luke 3:7; Rom. 2:5, 9:22; Phil. 2:12; Heb. 3:11. See William Ames' *Marrow of Theology* (Grand Rapids, MI: Baker Book house, 1998) 118.
[39] "Thou hast played the harlot with many lovers," (Jer. 3:1).
[40] "And it came to pass through the lightness of her whoredom, that she defiled the land, and committed adultery with stones and with stocks," (Jer. 3:9).
[41] "I am the LORD: that is my name: and my glory will I not give to another, neither my praise to graven images," (Isa. 42:8).
[42] "For the LORD thy God is a consuming fire, even a jealous God," (Deut. 4:24).

with their graven images," (Psa. 78:58). It's the absence of loveliness.

> "And he put forth the form of an hand, and took me by a lock of mine head; and the spirit lifted me up between the earth and the heaven, and brought me in the visions of God to Jerusalem, to the door of the inner gate that looketh toward the north; where was the seat of the image of jealousy, which provoketh to jealousy. 4 And, behold, the glory of the God of Israel was there, according to the vision that I saw in the plain. 5 Then said he unto me, Son of man, lift up thine eyes now the way toward the north. So I lifted up mine eyes the way toward the north, and behold northward at the gate of the altar this image of jealousy in the entry." (Ezek. 8:3).[43]

If that which is lovely is not upheld, mimicking the best being of all, *God*, God is jealous for that to be restored. That relationship needs to be mended, or it will face justice.[44]

---

[43] Deut. 32:16, 21; 1 Kings 14:22; Psalm 78:58; Ezek. 8:3-5.
[44] "Justice and judgment are the habitation of thy throne," (Psa. 89:14).

Chapter 1: Manasseh's Wickedness

The provoking sins of a man cannot compete with the nature of God; he is an all-consuming fire against sin.[45] Is it wise to anger an All-mighty God, a God of *all might?* Because God is holy and just, he must punish sin.[46] And because he must punish sin, he must of necessity by being provoked, execute a perfect hatred of sin which Scripture calls *his wrath*.[47] When justice is unleashed against sin, in wrath, such focused, direct, just and righteous power is directed against the one provoking him to sin; a mere man. They are getting far too close to the fire by obligation. Whether it is a nation, a church, a family, or an individual, God will get his justice. And it will be so fierce, that it will make one's ears tingle in simply hearing about that judgment.

What about the provoking sins of a nation? What could be said about that? "He did much evil in the sight of the LORD, to provoke Him to anger," (2 Kings 21:6). God brought, "calamity upon Jerusalem and Judah," (2 Kings 21:12). "So Manasseh seduced Judah and the inhabitants of Jerusalem," (2 Chron. 33:9). They were so deceived in their sin that they thought life

---

[45] Deut. 4:24, 9:3; Heb. 12:29.
[46] "The wicked shall not be unpunished," (Prov. 11:21).
[47] "For God hath not appointed us to wrath, but to obtain salvation by our Lord Jesus Christ, Who died for us, that, whether we wake or sleep, we should live together with him," (1 Thess. 5:9-10).

would just go on this way. People often think that God's silence in not bringing immediate wrath is somehow deficient on his part in judgment, or a future righteous judgment.[48] They fail to realize that God prepares them for the pit,[49] and does not just throw them into hell. He allows them to ripen in their sin. Puritan Daniel Williams said, "Security and impenitency is added to rebellion before God proceeds against a people."[50] He lets them stew in their rebellion in security and without the ability to repent because he doesn't grant it.[51] So, provoking sins can be of an entire nation against God. Such as a nation killing the fruit of its lust in abortion, killing their very children or tolerating iniquity of all kinds.

In the same way, especially in our passage, the church and the nation were one and the same; double

---

[48] "The Lord is not slack concerning his promise, as some men count slackness; but is longsuffering to us-ward, not willing that any should perish, but that all should come to repentance," (2 Peter 3:9).
[49] "Their foot shall slide in due time," (Deut. 32:35). "...to fill up their sins alway: for the wrath is come upon them to the uttermost," (1 Thess. 2:16).
[50] Nichols, J. *Puritan Sermons* Volume 4, (Wheaton, IL: Richard Owen Roberts, Publishers, 1981) 590; by Rev. Daniel Williams, D.D., in the sermon, What Repentance of National Sins Doth God Require as Ever We Expect National Mercies?
[51] "Ephraim is joined to idols: let him alone," (Hosea 4:17). "Therefore pray not thou for this people, neither lift up a cry or prayer for them: for I will not hear them in the time that they cry unto me for their trouble," (Jer. 11:14).

jeopardy. What does one do with the church in sin? Judah and the city of Jerusalem were, in fact, the church. They had the means of grace and did not only misuse them, but they *erased* them. There is no need to go over the abominable works of false worship, and the destruction of reformation again. Mediums? Witches? Sorcery? Burning their children alive? All of it was madness!

Provoking sins in a church can take many forms today, and in this case, they were all directed against worship, service, and godliness. Today, what is the difference between false worship that Manasseh gave his people, or some kind of false worship a wayward preacher gives his church? *False is false.* If the church will not serve God as he directs, is this so different? Is it even *more* heinous idolatry since it is against a professing Christ who *has* come? Is it a trampling of the Son of God underfoot?[52] Is that even worse than what Manasseh did? Are churches sacrificing their children on the altar of theological indifference and complacency.

---

[52] "Of how much sorer punishment, suppose ye, shall he be thought worthy, who hath trodden under foot the Son of God, and hath counted the blood of the covenant, wherewith he was sanctified, an unholy thing, and hath done despite unto the Spirit of grace?" (Heb. 10:29).

Theological error murders souls.[53] The godlessness of the people trickled down into even their personal lives, with personal gods, and such sins provoke an Almighty God to judgment. Is he not provoked today?

What about the provoking sins of a family? What would it take for a husband and wife to offer up their children to false gods, to burn them alive?[54] One really has to have a depraved heart and some devilish theological views to do that; offering up children in sacrifice to false gods and the devil. Today it is a little different. People become members of a church based on the youth group, or the kid's functions, that hundreds of thousands of families constantly do so that their kids aren't bored at church with no regard for what is true or false, what a church stands for or not. That translates today to *antibiblical views*. In other words, they choose a church because its close, it has a youth group, and it has activities for the kids. Expect for expunging their life in the fiery hands of a brass statue, how is this any different than in Manasseh's day? Parents are sacrificing

---

[53] "And Pharaoh said, Who is the LORD, that I should obey his voice to let Israel go? I know not the LORD, neither will I let Israel go," (Exod. 5:2). Pharaoh's heart in this was hardened, (Exodus 7:13; 14, 22, 8:15, 19, 32, 9:7, *etc.*).

[54] "There shall not be found among you any one that maketh his son or his daughter to pass through the fire," (Deut. 18:10).

their children on the altar of making them ignorant wretches.[55]

These provoking sins reached down to heads of households in families. It affects the way they deal with family worship and teaching their children each day, or not.[56] Whether they take the time to raise up a child in the way he should go. They never know when God might require their life and their 12-year-old son or daughter is then left to themselves. What will become of them (as if we need to ask that question to *Hezekiah*) at 12 years old? Little did Hezekiah know what would have become of Manasseh. Such sins of neglect provoke an Almighty God who takes careful notice of everything and judges each according to their works.[57]

And what of provoking sins of individuals? Provoking sins reach right down into the lives of the very individual.[58] Manasseh made an idol, to place it in the

---

[55] "Having the understanding darkened, being alienated from the life of God through the ignorance that is in them, because of the blindness of their heart," (Eph. 4:18).
[56] "...that they may learn to fear me all the days that they shall live upon the earth, and that they may teach their children," (Deut. 4:10).
[57] "Who without respect of persons judgeth according to every man's work," (1 Peter 1:17).
[58] "The soul that sinneth, it shall die. The son shall not bear the iniquity of the father, neither shall the father bear the iniquity of the son: the righteousness of the righteous shall be upon him, and the wickedness of the wicked shall be upon him," (Ezek. 18:20).

temple. "He even set a carved image, the idol which he had made, in the house of God," (2 Chron. 33:7). From great individuals, to the least individual, they all provoked him. They were all individually responsible; their sin changed their relationship with God. People are all individually responsible for their sin.

Provoking sins anger an Almighty God in nations, churches, families and the lives of individuals. And God will bring calamity on them if they do not repent. He'll do it when they are ripe for it, and it will be unmistakable. The Lord exercises his displeasure in the calamity of judgment on many who seemed to be professing Christians.[59] Many are given up to adultery, spiritual declension, ignorance, grievous sins of all kinds, even apostasy. Some might even say that they see in them a reprobate sense. It ought to be a great admonition to all Christians to look keenly at whether or not they tend to provoke God. Professing believers

---

[59] "And when thou prayest, thou shalt not be as the *hypocrites* are: for they love to pray standing in the synagogues and in the corners of the streets, that they may be seen of men. Verily I say unto you, They have their reward," (Matt. 6:5). See some instances of hypocrisy in the spies sent to entrap Jesus, Luke 20:21. Priests and Levites, Luke 10:31, 32. Chief priests, John 18:28. Ananias and Sapphira, Acts 5:1–10. Simon Magus, Acts 8:18–23. Peter and other Christians at Antioch, Gal. 2:11–14. Judaizing Christians in Galatia, Gal. 6:13. False teachers at Ephesus, Rev. 2:2.

must never provoke God. If they do, God will often humble them in some kind of coming calamity as he promised to Manasseh for his sin.

Provoking God leads to great "calamity." What are some provoking sins of the day? Consider the stretch of atheism across the land. People live as if there were no God or providence to govern the world.[60] They talk about great catastrophes in scientific terms of the weather, instead of judgment. Why do they do that?

Consider the vulgar immorality that stretches across the land; drunkenness, uncleanness, lying, backbiting, defrauding, irreligious swearing, false weights in matters of buying and selling, indifference in profaning the Lord's Day; and myriads of others. It is very easy to point to sins like these outside the church. But is the contemporary church exempt?[61] Is there an obstinate embrace to indifference to God's commands and Law? Is there an immoderate placement of the heart on worldliness and carnal gratification? Is there ignorance in the truth? Is there ignorance of Jesus Christ, the only way of salvation, of worship, of God's will exercised in godliness? Is there neglect of family

---

[60] "The fool hath said in his heart, There is no God," (Psa. 14:1).
[61] "For the time is come that judgment must begin at the house of God," (1 Peter 4:17).

worship? Is there unfruitfulness under all the means of grace? Is there spiritual declension in the lives of the ministers? Is there contempt in not attending on God's ordinances? Is there an establishing of one's own righteousness by religious duties? Do people profane baptism, the Lord's Supper? Is there a neglect of preparation to worship? John Willison said, do we "not keep up the impression of our sacramental vows, and of the matchless love of Christ displayed to us, so as to be thereby constrained to live to him that died for us, of not imitating the pattern of the holy Jesus, in his meekness, holiness, self-denial, mortification to the world, patience under wrongs, thankfulness for mercies, diligence in prayer, zeal for God s service, concern for the good of others, willingness to die, and resignation to God's will?"[62] Is there an ever-arching indifference to such things in the church?

How, then, do provoking sins come home to us? There is to be no rival to Jesus Christ and his kingdom in you or I as a covenanter, professing allegiance to Christ. The throne of Jesus Christ can have no rival with

---

[62] Willison, John, *The Whole Works of the Reverend and Learned John Willison*, Volume 2, (Edinburgh: J. Pillans and Sons, 1816) 472.

you as a believer.[63] Against idolatry God says, "I have sworn by Myself...That to Me every knee shall bow, every tongue shall take an oath," (Isa. 45:23). "...that at the name of Jesus every knee should bow, of those in heaven, and of those on earth, and of those under the earth, and that every tongue should confess that Jesus Christ is Lord, to the glory of God the Father." (Phil. 2:10-11). Christ cannot endure that the fear and reverence due to Him should be given to another, especially if you fabricate an idol of your own actions or thoughts. Indeed, this is idolatry and sacrilege to prefer the creature in any way before the Creator. Christ said, "If anyone comes to Me and does not hate his father and mother, wife and children, brothers and sisters, yes, and his own life also, he cannot be My disciple," (Luke 14:26). You must have a love to Christ that exceeds all things which is necessary to escape the curse at his coming. Material or immaterial, things or thoughts, all of them are required to be in subjection to Christ.

How might we tell if our "all" is not given to Christ? Measure your time with them. Consider what

---

[63] "If any man come to me, and hate not his father, and mother, and wife, and children, and brethren, and sisters, yea, and his own life also, he cannot be my disciple," (Luke 14:26).

you love most.⁶⁴ Christ's displeasure can turn to righteous anger when we, as Christians, give our love and devotion to another, like a spiritual harlot, to some type of pretended god, even if it is the self. Any such challenge to God's rightful claim provokes His wrath and kindles His jealousy for His name.

Christ will have no rival, or God will be provoked by your sins. Though Christ is meek and lowly of heart, and he demonstrates a meekness about himself and among us, yet if we provoke him, we shall know that he can show himself as a Lion, and as a consuming fire, as he describes himself, "One that hath feet like burning brass, out of whose mouth proceeds a fiery sword," (Revelation 1:15). If Christ is our God, neither death nor life must separate us from him. We must let the things of life go which may hinder us in our walk with God, rather than that our God should leave. Thomas Boston said, "All the Lord's people are not martyrs in action, but all are martyrs in resolution. Whatever we do or suffer for God, we must beware we put it not in Christ's room, for he will endure no rival. We must renounce our

---

[64] "Love not the world, neither the things that are in the world. If any man love the world, the love of the Father is not in him," (1 John 2:15).

confidence in all, as if we had done nothing."[65] He will have no rival in your heart. He will reside there, will be the Word of God there, will provoke you to good works there, will deposit his Spirit there, and he and the Father will dwell with you.[66] Only vain men detract from the sufficiency of the Scripture, and mingle their own or other men's inventions with divine institutions. Is this not what Manasseh did? Christ will allow no rival in anything that he has ownership of in your soul.

You might say, "but do we really set up idols like Manasseh today?" No, no...*ours are worse*. How long did God allow Manasseh and the people to sin? Years. We get complacent in sins we don't even know we commit, or we become brazen to commit sins willfully which we know God hates, time after time. And how do we handle that? We tend to quote Scripture, "I am carnal, sold under sin. For what I am doing, I do not understand. For what I will to do, that I do not practice; but what I hate, that I do," (Rom. 7:14-15). We think, *oh well, this is just the way things are until we get to heaven*. You see, reader, it's the "Oh well" that is provoking to him.

---

[65] Boston, Thomas, *The Whole Works of the Late Reverend Thomas Boston*, Volume 2, (Aberdeen: George and Robert King, 1848) 98.
[66] "Jesus answered and said unto him, If a man love me, he will keep my words: and my Father will love him, and we will come unto him, and make our abode with him," (John 14:23).

I don't wish to exasperate you on this point, but I do want you to faithfully understand it without crumbling under its weight. When professing believers sin, they sin worse than the devil, for they sin against the broken body and shed blood of Christ.[67] The devil does not do that; but when you sin against him in any manner, as professing Christ, you do that. How do you Provoke God worse than Manasseh did? By not cherishing the blessings Christ gives you while you have them. Manasseh was all about instant gratification. What can guide me, help me, aid me, direct me right now. He was not waiting for God at any point. Everything he instituted was some kind of attempt at discerning what the future holds, what he was going to be blessed with later on. He did not cherish anything.

You can provoke God in trying to control every aspect of your life. Manasseh did this through his attempted witchcraft. The biblical idea of witchcraft is *manipulation*. Trying to do all one can to manipulate the circumstances of an event, not submitting under God's providence. When you want to be master and

---

[67] "Of how much sorer punishment, suppose ye, shall he be thought worthy, who hath trodden under foot the Son of God, and hath counted the blood of the covenant, wherewith he was sanctified, an unholy thing, and hath done despite unto the Spirit of grace?" (Heb. 10:29).

commander over the Lord Jesus who is the Master and the Commander, you provoke him.

You often, like Manasseh, set up *self* over God. You tend to mistake idolatry for mere visibility of strange objects and idols, when it is really an issue of the heart. *Idolatry is a heart issue.* Manasseh was selfish in every way. What do you love most? What does your life show you love most? Cars, hobbies, family, school, work? If you spend 3 hours with your hobby each day and 15 minutes with God, what do you, practically speaking, love *more*? If the Christian religion is what you do on Sundays for an hour or two, or what you feel you are forced to do during the week, what else takes up your time that you love most? What is most important? Carnal self-love is loving yourself over everything else. All things are attempted to bend to your own will. The root of sin is self-love because men love themselves more than they love God. Those who are spiritually intemperate are drunk with pride, or covetousness, or passions; they are filled with love of their pleasures and ease, with love of the world and the things in the world. That cannot coexist with the love of God, and it makes a rival of Christ in your heart. Again, 1 John 2:15 says, "Do not love the world or the things in the world. If anyone loves the world, the love of the Father is not in him." Self-love makes your heart long after the world, not fixed on God and heavenly things, but hurried about with ceaseless business. Look at the creativity of Manasseh in such things. He was pleasing himself instead of God. What kind of time was lost? Robert Leighton said, "it is a most unseemly and unpleasant thing, to see a man's life full of ups and downs, one step like a Christian, and another like a worldling; it cannot choose but both pain himself and mar the edification of others."[68]

Is there a way, then, to stop provoking and angering an Almighty God?[69] For you, it is to have no other rival in your life than God through Jesus Christ. "Yet indeed I also count all things loss for the excellence of the knowledge of Christ Jesus my Lord, for whom I have suffered the loss of all things, and count them as rubbish, that I may gain Christ and be found in Him," (Phil. 3:8-11); no other rival, no provoking sin. Christ is *all*, and he says to you, "without me you can do nothing."

Christ suffered for all your provoking sins. The lust, the wandering eye, the profaning of Lord's Day, the

---

[68] Leighton, Robert, *The Whole Works of Robert Leighton*, Volume 1, (London: Hatchard and Son, 1828) 179.
[69] "The time is fulfilled, and the kingdom of God is at hand: repent ye, and believe the gospel," (Mark 1:15).

neglect of personal daily devotions to God, the constant neglect of family, addictions of all kinds, the bottle, the needle, the pill, the money hungry, despondency, pride, hate, the neglect of holy duties, the despising of biblical worship, pick whatever is a bosom sin! How are you to think about this? God beckons you as if he were to say:

> Get rid of all your sins, through my Son. You have professed love to me. But you provoke me in your sin. I have given you my Word time and time again. I have declared it to you in Christ concerning my heart. Do you not see it here written, "Go and sin no more?" Do you count that lightly? My Son endured the stable as a birth place for His kingship, the weakness of human flesh as the manner of upholding My will, to be smitten, afflicted, burden and cast down, even to have no place to rest his head. He was abused by scoffers and pagans and soldiers, and He is the Lord of Glory. I had him willingly offer himself for sin, willingly give himself for all your provoking sins, and yet you continue to sin. Why do you call me Lord, Lord and do not do the things which I say? Do you not think I am truly

serious about sin? Do you not think that your sins no longer provoke me, or grieve me or anger me? My Son gave up his life to die for sin. He is the Only begotten, full of grace and truth and life and power, and yet he gave of himself for your besetting sins, secret sins, evil sins you still hold in your heart. You sneer at Manasseh and shake your head thinking you are not like him? "But who maketh thee to differ?" You must be serious about sin, and radical about sin, if you are to be my disciple. You must take up your cross, and follow my Son. You must take this seriously. My Son never said to you, "do your best." He said you are to be perfect as I am perfect. Why? My Word speaks clearly, "He who is born of God doth not sin." The one born of my Spirit, indwelt with my Spirit does not make a habitual life of sin to revel in it and provoke me. Do not provoke me Christian. Do you not know that my glittering sword against sin is sharp, where my hand shall take hold of vengeance for my name and glory, and make you know what it means in Scripture to "provoke the Lord to jealousy," for I the Lord do not change, and as Manasseh provoked me in

Chapter 1: Manasseh's Wickedness

his sin, so all your sins provoke me as well if you continue in them.

Reader, do you despair in this? Christ answers for you:

Stop your hand Father! Hold back on that justice. Those sins that you speak of, you know, you decreed, you taught in Scripture, they are transferred to another. They are transferred to me. They are on my account. I have taken their wrath for all those sins. Those souls will not be treated as sons of darkness, but sons and daughters of light. They must not die, for they are no longer guilty of them. Yes, Lord, the debt was great, but I have undertaken the eternal covenant to pay it all. Where they have provoked you to anger, where they have provoked you to jealousy, where you are wronged O God, all of it was placed completely on my account. I went to the cross and offered myself there for life and godliness, that they may taste and see that the Lord is good and live a victorious life walking in the power of my Spirit which I send to them from my throne of authority, which you gave me. I

> resolved to be their Surety, I was content to be made that offering for them. Though I knew no sin, though I was never in the least bit guilty, I took it all for them. And I love them, for while they were yet sinners, I died for them. You pressed your sharp sword into my heart for them, I was wounded, bruised, chastised, and afflicted by your wrath. Wherever you found sin in them, I took their sin, and it was imputed to me, for I know you could not forbear to punish it. You punished me thoroughly for their provoking sins. And I know, you Father, agree with me in this.

Then Christ speaks to you in all this:

> I took the justice, stripes, and beating for you, I sweat blood on the ground in prayer for you. When the Father had forsaken me as I hung cursed on the tree, he did not spare anything. I willingly was wounded for all your provoking sins, all your besetting sins, all your presumptuous sins, all your secret faults. I did this so you would be brought closer to God, your

wounds would be closed and cured by the balm of my precious saving ointment. That all my benefits would be applied to your souls. I was very willing to see the travail of my soul to undergo the curse, that you may receive the blessing, even eternal life. That you may be assisted by my Spirit in sanctification, and put off provoking sins before My Father's face. I changed you, converted you, gave you faith to believe, and I indwell you. I fill you up by my Spirit. Do not grieve him. Do not quench him. Take seriously my Father's Law, my Father's glory, my Fathers holiness; take seriously what I did even for Manasseh, what I did for you. Is there any sin that is too great for me to forgive? Is there any sin so strong that it cannot be overcome by my blood? Are you more of a sinner than I am a Savior? I saved you so that you would be happy in holiness. I died...that you may live.

A billion trillion *Manasseh's* and their sin could not squelch the work of the Anointed Redeemer.[70] But that

---

[70] "But this man, after he had offered one sacrifice for sins for ever, sat down on the right hand of God," (Heb. 10:12).

never gives us a license to sin. Shall we go on sinning that such a grace as this might more abound to us? Certainly not. Do not imitate Manasseh in self-love. Do not make Manasseh your father. Self-love is misery. Christ is a loving Savior, but do not be deceived thinking that Christ is simply a get out of jail free card. To God, sin is never a game.[71] Do not provoke him, knowing that Christ took the plunge of the sword on your behalf, and he was dealt the blow of death and hell so you don't have to.

But be warned, that if you live a life which continues to provoke God willingly, without remorse, without repentance, without holiness, you show yourself to be a mere professor of religion, and not a true son or daughter. Religion like that is on the tongue but far from the heart. Manasseh was like that for most of his life. We will find, though, later, that God changed him.

Christ will have no rival in your heart. Never be caught under his warnings.[72] God Almighty says to such that continue to provoke him, "Behold, I am bringing

---

[71] "How then can I do this great wickedness, and sin against God?" (Gen. 39:9).
[72] "Repent; or else I will come unto thee quickly, and will fight against them with the sword of my mouth," (Rev. 2:16).

such calamity...that whoever hears of it, both his ears will tingle," (2 Kings 21:12), because provoking sins, anger the Almighty God.

Chapter 2:
Manasseh's Wickedness Part 2

"He even set a carved image, the idol which he had made, in the house of God, of which God had said to David and to Solomon his son, "In this house and in Jerusalem, which I have chosen out of all the tribes of Israel, I will put My name forever; and I will not again remove the foot of Israel from the land which I have appointed for your fathers-- only if they are careful to do all that I have commanded them, according to the whole law and the statutes and the ordinances by the hand of Moses," (2 Chronicles 33:7-10).

Covenant stipulations are always given to covenant people. "You shall have no other gods before Me," (Exod. 20:3). "You shall not make for yourself a carved image," (Exod. 20:4). "You shall not take the name of the LORD your God in vain," (Exod. 20:7). "Remember the Sabbath day, to keep it holy." (Exod. 20:8). In these commandments, the first table of the Law, we find the object, means, manner, and time of worship. Central to this idea is what God says in 2 Chronicles 33:7, where "My name" will be there. God says that he will put his name in the midst of his covenant people, forever. God's name is eternally placed in Christ. It is in the temple here in 2 Chronicles, but after the types and shadows of the Old Testament are done away with, it is the temple of the body, the temple of the Holy Spirit, where God's name dwells forever.

God's name and his commands not only give his people blessings, but the rejection of those commands, or sin against them, have penal sanctions. If they are kept, one will be blessed.[1] If they are abused, one will be judged, and cursed. *The Westminster Larger Catechism* in question 112, says concerning the third commandment, it requires, "that the name of God, his titles, attributes, ordinances, the word, sacraments, prayer, oaths, vows, lots, his works, and whatsoever else there is by which he makes himself known, be holily and reverently used in thought, meditation, word, and writing; by a holy profession, and answerable conversation, to the glory of God, and the good of ourselves, and others." God's name, the name of the Lord, in various phrases is found hundreds of times throughout Scripture. God's word, being and attributes

---

[1] "Blessed shalt thou be when thou comest in, and blessed shalt thou be when thou goest out," (Deut. 28:6).

are all attached to his name; they are all one and the same. His name is power. "For "whoever calls on the name of the LORD shall be saved," (Rom. 10:13). "That at the name of Jesus every knee should bow," (Phil. 2:10). God promised to place his name of power, his name of *saving* power, in the midst of the people forever, if they would obey him, if they are careful to do all that God required. Manasseh *was not careful* to do anything God required, and instead, set up the exact opposite to everything that God instructed him as a king leading his people before the face of God and according to the Law.

God said that there will be a special place that He would dwell with his people.[2] In this special place of Judah, in the midst of the city of peace, in a specially built temple, which cannot contain him, yet, there, he promises to put his name on it. What a wonderful name it is. Christians can no more find out the depths of God's name to perfection, than they can his nature and essence. Both his name, and his essence are infinite and unsearchable. God says, "Why askest thou thus after my name, seeing it is wonderful?" (Judges 13:18). Christ's

---

[2] "And they shall put my name upon the children of Israel; and I will bless them," (Num. 6:27). "I have hallowed this house, which thou hast built, to put my name there for ever; and mine eyes and mine heart shall be there perpetually," (1 Kings 9:3).

Chapter 2: Manasseh's Wickedness Part 2

name, the Anointed Messiah, has the name above every name, which is *the Lord*.³ His name is *Wonderful*, as Isaiah 9:6 says.

God's name is attached to the cursing and the warning. The people must be careful to do all that he has commanded them according to, literally, "all the law". His name is attached closely to his word, to the Law, because the Law is a reflection of who God is. Violate the word, and one has violated the name of God. God sees a violation of the Word as trampling his good name. He won't stand for that. A violation of the moral Law of God is a capital offense. *Forever* it is a capital offense. Break that capital offense and *the wages of sin is death*. Lying is a capital offense. Idolatry is a capital offense. Disregarding the Lord's Day is a capital offense. Violating God's good name is a capital offense.

Verse 9 says, "So Manasseh seduced Judah and the inhabitants of Jerusalem to do more evil than the nations whom the LORD had destroyed before the children of Israel." The Word "seduced" is literally, "caused to wander." This is likened to placing people

---

³ "That at the name of Jesus every knee should bow, of things in heaven, and things in earth, and things under the earth; And that every tongue should confess that Jesus Christ *is Lord*, to the glory of God the Father," (Phil. 2:10-11).

within a drunken stupor. He caused them to be lead into error. Caused them to do evil. Caused them to be in a stupor. They were not of a right mind, were drunk with evil and in a wicked daze.

Not only did they *do* evil, but they did *more* evil than the surrounding nations; and those nations did not know God. Manasseh sinned against his kingly office in every respect. He restored idolatry and destroyed the reformation under Hezekiah his father. He blasphemed God to his face, erecting idols in God's sanctuary. He made a covenant with the devil in witchcraft, Spiritism and such, selling his soul. He was a murderer of people and souls. And he continued in this for many years, many decades! He did it better and more zealously and with more creativity than all the other pagan nations combined since the history of the world. Francis Roberts called Manasseh, "a prodigious monster of wickedness."[4] Thomas Brooks called him, "a monstrous devil incarnate."[5] There are very few people in the history of the Word who deserve that title as it is so spoken. Yet, aren't all sinners of this kind against the

---

[4] Roberts, Francis, *The Mystery and Marrow of the Bible*, (London: R.W., 1657) 1089.
[5] Brooks, Thomas, *The Works of Thomas Brooks*, Volume 1, (London: James Nisbet, 1866) 143.

Lord Jesus Christ monstrous devils of wickedness? "If ye [*that's you reader*] then, being *evil*, know how to give good gifts unto your children, how much more shall your Father which is in heaven give good things to them that ask him?" (Matt. 7:11). Jesus calls *all men evil.*

Verse 10 reads, "And the LORD spoke to Manasseh and his people, but they would not listen." 2 Kings 21:10 says, "And the LORD spoke by His servants the prophets." Stubbornness against godly admonitions is a very serious sin. God spoke to Manasseh and his people, but they would not listen or amend their ways. It is not as though he got a letter in the mail. He did not get advice from one of his counselors. God specifically sent ministers to him to preach the Word to him and he threw it off. Romans 1:18 gives the expression, "children of stubbornness, on whom wrath comes," which is very applicable here. These are those sinners who cannot be persuaded to leave their sins and seek God by true faith and repentance.[6] These are children of disobedience and rebellion. William Ames said, "Such men's condition is most desperate, because they are not only sinners, but

---

[6] "They ceased not from their own doings, nor from their stubborn way," (Judges 2:19).

also stubborn in their sins."[7] They are shown in the book of Romans as those whose condition is to be abhorred, and whose example and company is to be shunned, as appears from verse 7, "therefore do not be partakers," *etc.* Why? Because men like this, or even women like this, serve as slaves to the devil himself, who is their master; they serve the father of lies, and they are bound and serve sin. Such stubbornness is seen in Pharaoh in the time of Moses, "And Pharaoh said, "Who is the LORD, that I should obey His voice to let Israel go? I do not know the LORD, nor will I let Israel go," (Exod. 5:2). It is as if Manasseh said, "I know God, and I've been taught all about him. I have the law, I have the prophets, they are even bringing me messages from God; but you know what, I don't care. I don't care what my father taught me growing up. I don't care about God's name. I don't care what God says in his word. I don't care what his ministers tell me, past or present. I don't care what the Law says. I don't care what God says, period. I'm going to act, live and believe whatever suits me." Slaves of human depravity in this way are always ready to rebel

---

[7] Ames, William, *The Substance of Religion*, (London: T. Mabb, 1659) 25.

against Divine authority.[8] They do so every chance they can, and they are stubborn in it.

Manasseh also takes much of the blame here for the people not listening. He caused them to err; he seduced them. He caused them to do evil. He told them, "don't listen to God's word. Don't' listen to the ministers and messengers he sends to you. Don't listen to a godly heritage. Don't listen to any of it – just listen to what I've been telling you; what I have is better." And he got away with it for decades, or so he thought.

Those who dissuade others from hearing the preaching of true ministers are *evil.* They build and heap up even on themselves the sins of others. Manasseh had heaped upon on his own sins, even the sins of other men. He not only lead the people by his example, but compelled them by his commands making them to act worse than the heathen God had rooted out of the land. In this he is credited with the guilt of the whole nation on himself. And, he continued in it even though God spoke to him, told him the truth, told him to repent, through his prophets. Manasseh's life is a complete mess, and a total rebellion against God.

---

[8] "The haters of the LORD should have submitted themselves unto him," (Psa. 81:15). "Haters of God," (Rom. 1:30).

It is not hard to understand that sinning against the knowledge of God is sinning against God's mercy. Consider first the relationship between sinning and the knowledge of God. What does it mean to *sin against knowledge*? I do not want to deal with those ignorant of the ways of God in the doctrine, but with "covenant bound" Manasseh. These are people who have the light of the knowledge of God, and yet, sin against it. This means we are dealing with *people in the church*. This means we deal with people who have *tasted* the Holy Spirit, and the good things of the age to come.[9] This means we deal with people who hear preaching, and, do many religious duties. This doctrine for them means, that, since God has given his people his revealed will in the Word, they are expected to know it and obey it. So, to sin against it, is to sin against his condescension, it is to sin against his mercy. In his condescension, God covenanted with Christ, the Lord of glory, to save souls. In his condescension, he sent the Christ to come and die on a cross, giving up his life, and reckoning his righteousness to all believers. This covenant of God's grace is not to be taken lightly. To sin against the

---

[9] "And have tasted the good word of God, and the powers of the world to come," (Heb. 6:5).

covenant of God is even a greater sin than to sin against a single commandment of God, or to sin against a single promise, or to sin against a single ordinance.[10] Where there is more mercy, there is more sin. There is more mercy in God's covenant with Christ than anything else. Commandments *tell* people their duty (which they ought to obey), but those commandments spoken or preached do not give them *any power* to fulfill their duty. It is only through the covenant of grace which gives power to do what it requires to be done, and that through Jesus Christ and his work, as well as his sending the Spirit to produce fruits of righteousness in people. Edmund Calamy said, "If it be a hell-procuring sin to break the least of God's commandments, how much more to be a covenant breaker?"[11] This is a greater sin than to sin even against a mere promise of God. This covenant is a promise joined together with the Christ, and his work, and his power, and his Spirit. It is joined in the immutable decree of God's perpetual and

---

[10] "As I live, surely mine oath that he hath despised, and my covenant that he hath broken, even it will I recompense upon his own head," (Ezek. 17:19).

[11] McMahon, C. Matthew, Editor, *The Covenanted Reformation*, A Sermon at London by Rev. Edmund Calamy, (Coconut Creek, FL: Puritan Publications, 2009) 299.

everlasting oath.[12] It is not merely a promise of things guaranteed, but it is bound by God's *unchangeableness*. Manasseh's sin was a great affront to covenant breaking and evil in light of all God instructed in his condescension to save his people. Even the amount of light Manasseh had at his time was still of great measure. So many prophets, so many words, so much direction, so much condescension by God to stoop and deliver messages to a monstrous devil like him. So many preachers, so many churches, so many professing Christians through the world today, yet, where is the revival? Are there no revivals? Are there no awakenings? In his mercy, believers are to know God's mind. God set down the rules of holiness that demonstrate his character in the word. If one wishes to be like God, they follow his Law and his statues. This is the very thing Manasseh rejected in verse 8 – because he was not careful to do all that God commanded him.[13] He had no desire to be like God.[14] He had no desire to take God at his word. It is one thing to sin in ignorance, or with little

---

[12] "Wherein God, willing more abundantly to shew unto the heirs of promise the immutability of his counsel, confirmed it by an oath," (Heb. 6:17).

[13] "Ye shall observe to do therefore as the LORD your God hath commanded you: ye shall not turn aside to the right hand or to the left," (Deut. 5:32).

[14] "Be ye therefore followers of God, as dear children," (Eph. 5:1).

light, against the law written on the heart and conscience as the heathen nations did. What makes professing covenant members worse in *their* sin? They sin against knowledge delivered directly to them by Jesus Christ. It is the Spirit's job to illuminate the mind. "Open thou mine eyes, that I may behold wondrous things out of thy law," (Psa. 119:18). Manasseh had that instruction in the Psalms. It was incumbent on him to pray for the Spirit of divine illumination, to have that supernatural and divine light.[15]

Manasseh did more evil than the heathen nations, not because his actions were more heinous, but because the actions were committed in light of having the knowledge of God. Pagans sacrificed their children to Molech in the fire. Manasseh did too. What they did he did. But can there be a level of his sin verses their sin? It was not simply by extent, but by the *context* of that sin. He had this, for example: "But the person who does anything presumptuously, whether he is native-born or a stranger, that one brings reproach on the LORD, and he shall be cut off from among his people. 'Because he has despised the Word of the LORD, and has broken His

---

[15] "Thy word is a lamp unto my feet, and a light unto my path," (Psa. 119:105). "Open thou mine eyes, that I may behold wondrous things out of thy law," (Psa. 119:18).

commandment, that person shall be completely cut off; his guilt shall be upon him.'" (Num. 15:30-31). Does not Christ say, "For everyone to whom much is given, from him much will be required;" (Luke 12:48). The more knowledge of God, the more sin. More knowledge is more guilt. Manasseh should have been praying that God would illumine his intellect that he may behold wondrous things out of the law. He should have sparked in his will a great desire to hear what God would say to him. Instead, opposite to having a great love for the Word of God, he had a contempt and despising of the divine Word (Jer. 6:10; 8:9; Amos 2:1; Matt. 23:27; 2 Chron. 36:16). He had a hatred of it (Job 21:14). He plugged his ears to it (Psa. 58:4-5). He avoided it (Job 21:14; Num. 21:5; Prov. 3:11). Utterly neglected it (Jer. 18:18; 19:15; Zeph. 3:2). And was stiff-necked toward it with great resistance (Acts 13:45).[16] God says that sinning against him in such wickedness is so heinous that anyone who hears about God's judgments against people who commit such sins, *both his ears will tingle.*

When someone sins in ignorance, there is a certain level of judgment against that sin. When there is a sin based on knowledge then there is always *more guilt*

---

[16] *cf.* Acts 13:46 and Rev. 2:5.

based on the light that men have of the word. This places the Christian in a precarious position because they have the whole word of God to look to. They never have the excuse of sinning in ignorance. They must know the word.[17] They must do the word. "But be ye doers of the word, and not hearers only, deceiving your own selves," (James 1:22). Jesus likened such doers *wise* who built their house on the rock. Manasseh did all he could to reject what God said, to extinguish all light from the kingdom, in order to sin more freely for his own benefit, and he propagated unbiblical opinions over the truth. On top of that, he did it *creatively*.

Sinning against the knowledge of God is to sin against God's name. God will never allow continued sin against His name. It is first based on the majesty of God. God is a jealous God for His own glory and majesty. Exodus 34:14, "For you shall worship no other god, for the LORD, whose name is Jealous, is a jealous God." God cannot deny his supreme majesty. 2 Timothy 2:13 says, "If we are faithless, He remains faithful; He cannot deny Himself." He must punish wickedness due to His majestic nature, for everything opposed to him must of

---

[17] "These were more noble than those in Thessalonica, in that they received the word with all readiness of mind, and searched the scriptures daily, whether those things were so," (Acts 17:11).

necessity be eternally punished. Then consider adding *holiness* to God's name. His name is holy. Everything attached to his name is holy. That means his Word is holy.[18] Christ, the Word, is the Holy one of Israel.[19] He is the one without spot or blemish, the accepted Son of God's love who Redeems by way of his perfect life, death and resurrection.[20] He sends, from his intercessory throne of grace to sinners the Holy Spirit. "...that God would give you His Holy Spirit." His worship is holy. His statues and laws and judgments about all things good for the Christian are holy. When a professing believer then sins against God to do his own thing and go his own way and believes whatever he wants, a holy God cannot be peaceably joined to that. Satisfaction must be made to his justice. Either, Christ will be that satisfaction through their repentance, or they might begin their path of trampling the Son of God underfoot,

---

[18] "Therefore as the fire devoureth the stubble, and the flame consumeth the chaff, so their root shall be as rottenness, and their blossom shall go up as dust: because they have cast away the law of the LORD of hosts, and despised the word of the Holy One of Israel," (Isa. 5:24).

[19] "Wherefore he saith also in another psalm, Thou shalt not suffer thine Holy One to see corruption," (Acts 13:35).

[20] "Forasmuch as ye know that ye were not redeemed with corruptible things, as silver and gold, from your vain conversation received by tradition from your fathers; But with the precious blood of Christ, as of a lamb without blemish and without spot," (1 Peter 1:18-19).

or they will be catechized and visited by God with his corrective and frowning providences. It is not appropriate to the holiness of God to cultivate a friendship with someone who defiles His name, so long as he *continues in* defiling his name.[21] This kind of person is called a covenant breaker whom God rejects. God says upon which he will bring calamity. Mercy is seen in condescension, in the covenant taken to uphold God's Name.

What is a covenant?[22] A covenant is a pact or agreement between two parties.[23] This is a vow, binds the parties to the oath. In this case it is God and man. I will put my name...on them. In response, without a solemn vow to God in the things of religion people are

---

[21] "And ye shall be holy unto me: for I the LORD am holy," (Lev. 20:26).

[22] "Incline your ear, and come unto me: hear, and your soul shall live; and I will make an everlasting covenant with you, even the sure mercies of David," (Isa. 55:3).

[23] Examples of *covenant* are of the sabbath, Exod. 31:16. Of the Ten Commandments, Exod. 34:28; Deut. 5:2, 3; 9:9. With Adam, Gen. 2:16, 17; Noah, Gen. 8:16; 9:8-17; Abraham, Gen. 12:1-3; 15; 17:1-22; Exod. 6:4-8; Psa. 105:8-11; Rom. 9:7-13; Gal. 3. With Isaac, Gen. 17:19; Jacob, Gen. 28:13-15. With the Israelites to deliver them from Egypt, Exod. 6:4-8. With Phinehas, Num. 25:12, 13. With Israel, at Horeb, Deut. 5:2, 3; in Moab, Deut. 29:1-15. Of the Levites, Neh. 13:29; Mal. 2:4, 5. With David, 2 Sam. 7:12-16; 1 Chron. 17:11-14; 2 Chron. 6:16. With David and his house, 2 Sam. 23:5; Psa. 89:20-37; Jer. 33:21. With his people, Isa. 55:3; 59:21. The fulfillment of the covenant in Christ, Jer. 31:31-34; Heb. 8:4-13; Heb. 12:18-24; Heb. 13:20.

just full of "talk". It is just religiosity. Theology held in the heart must incorporate godly action. Deuteronomy 6:4-6, "Hear, O Israel: The LORD our God, the LORD is one! You shall love the LORD your God with all your heart, with all your soul, and with all your strength. And these words which I command you today shall be in your heart." Can this be any plainer? The church, in any age, then, in its desire to follow God and Christ, is bound to oath and vow before the living God to fulfill its task. That is the basic duty of all Christians in loving God. To uphold the knowledge of God in Word and deed. "For this is the love of God, that we keep his commandments: and his commandments are not grievous," (1 John 5:3). The reality surrounding the greatest commandment to love God with all your heart and mind demonstrates that lawful oaths are central to a true confession by any Christian! That is why God was so angry and provoked at Manasseh's sin. The covenant community was being led astray to things contrary to the place where God had placed his name.

How could a Christian, truly be on the road of sanctification without a solemn resolve, a binding resolve, to uphold the Word of God in their walk? He is a hypocrite who thinks he can do so without an oath or vow.[24] He is a pretender (which is what the Greek connotation of what "hypocrite" means). "Whosoever taketh an oath ought duly to consider the weightiness of so solemn an act, and therein to avouch nothing but what he is fully persuaded is the truth."[25] Christians can agree that a godly life is good, and necessary, but unless they are taking advantage of the time God gives them to enact it, then it is simply theory. What good are theories never lived out? For when a Christian sins against God, he sins not only against the commandment but against the covenant he's in with God. In every sin he commits, he is a commandment-breaker, and a covenant-breaker.[26] In this God sees his name as defiled.[27]

How long will Christ endure that without chastising his sons and daughters? God is always against

---

[24] "Thou shalt fear the LORD thy God, and serve him, and shalt swear by his name," (Deut. 6:13). "Again, ye have heard that it hath been said by them of old time, Thou shalt not forswear thyself, but shalt perform unto the Lord thine oaths," (Matt. 5:33).
[25] *1647 Westminster Confession of Faith* 22:3.
[26] "My covenant will I not break, nor alter the thing that is gone out of my lips," (Psa. 89:34).
[27] Sins which make the times perilous are: "For men shall be lovers of their own selves, covetous, boasters, proud, blasphemers, disobedient to parents, unthankful, unholy, Without natural affection, trucebreakers, false accusers, incontinent, fierce, despisers of those that are good, Traitors, heady, highminded, lovers of pleasures more than lovers of God; Having a form of godliness, but denying the power thereof: from such turn away." (2 Tim. 3:2-5).

covenant breaking. Joshua said, "Ye cannot serve the LORD: for he is an holy God; he is a jealous God; he will not forgive your transgressions nor your sins. If ye forsake the LORD, and serve strange gods, then he will turn and do you hurt, and consume you, after that he hath done you good," (Josh. 24:19-20). Manasseh did not only break covenant with God as a covenant-breaker. He desecrated it. He entered into the lowest depths of sin possible. He took it to the highest level he could, and that with ingenuity.

    Professing Christians often sin against the knowledge of God. The reason is that they do not heed or know God's word.[28] After Manasseh initially committed so many inwardly and outwardly heinous sins, his judgment on those sins were equally aggravated to include the wickedness of not listening to God after the sinning started. God in his gracious disposition sent heralds with a message to Manasseh. The tempting of the Lord by Manasseh and the people of Judah is recorded by the Chronicler in such a way to be somewhat repetitive that the reader becomes aggravated at the degeneracy of the sin given in the

---

[28] "But if any man be ignorant, let him be ignorant," (1 Cor. 14:38). "For this they willingly are ignorant," (2 Peter 3:5).

narrative. But regardless if it is a total desecration of the covenant, or simply the beginnings of covenant breaking, all of it surrounds *not listening to God.* Take that idea down to its simple root – it was simply not listening to what God said.[29] Even in the midst of the height of their worst sins, God still reaches down to them in grace. God is infinitely amazing in his mercy to reach down into the filthiest mire possible with wicked sinners and still send them a message to listen to for the good of their repentance. He sends people the word; in the beginning was the word, the Word is God, the Word is his name, his name is holy and placed on the people. This is the Christ sent, who comes as the Son of Man to exegete the Father and show the world the love of the Father, and the way to true happiness. God does this, whether in the Old Testament or New Testament by his messengers, his heralds, his ministers. "How beautiful upon the mountains are the feet of him who brings good news, Who proclaims peace, Who brings glad tidings of good things, Who proclaims salvation, Who says to

---

[29] "My people are destroyed for lack of knowledge: because thou hast rejected knowledge, I will also reject thee, that thou shalt be no priest to me: seeing thou hast forgotten the law of thy God, I will also forget thy children," (Hos. 4:6).

Zion, "Your God reigns!"'" (Isa. 52:7). But will people *listen*?

Sinning against the knowledge of God is sinning against God's *mercy*. In Jesus Christ is found infinite loftiness and infinite condescension. Both are present in the God-man. This is what Isaiah saw in Isa. 6:1-4. There Christ was, high, lofty, and lifted up. Who would have thought that such a high, lofty and lifted up Christ would stoop to save? He is infinitely great and high above everything, with nothing his rival. He is higher than kings like Manasseh. He is the King of kings and Lord of lords. He is higher than angels, higher than Moses, as the book of Hebrews instructs. He is infinitely beyond the reach and scope of any men. Men cannot reach up to him. They have no power to move heavenward. His very name is wonderful; it is past the comprehension of men. In this, Christ is the sovereign Lord of all. He is the Son of Man, the divine God, ruling over all creation and all men in all ages. He is without limits of any kind. And as he is infinite in being, infinite in loftiness, so he is infinite in the actions of his being, infinite in mercy to his people. He is infinite in every way.[30] He is infinite in his condescension; he is infinite in his stooping to save.

Jonathan Edwards said,

> "None are so low or inferior, but Christ's condescension is sufficient to take a gracious notice of them. He condescends not only to the angels, humbling himself to behold the things that are done in heaven, but he also condescends to such poor creatures as men; and that not only so as to take notice of princes and great men, but of those that are of meanest rank and degree, the, "poor of the world," James 2:5. Such as are commonly despised by their fellow creatures, Christ does not despise. 1 Cor. 1:28, "Base things of the world, and things that are despised, hath God chosen." Christ condescends to take notice of beggars, Luke 16:22, and of servants, and people of the most despised nations: in Christ Jesus is neither "Barbarian, Scythian, bond nor free," Col. 3:11. He that is in this way high, condescends to take a gracious notice of little

---

[30] "Great is our Lord, and of great power: his understanding is infinite," (Psa. 147:5).

children. Matt. 19:14, "Suffer little children to come unto me." Yes, what is much more, his condescension is sufficient to take a gracious notice of the most unworthy, sinful creatures, those that have infinite ill deservings."[31]

The Lord Jesus is high and lofty and lifted up, and he stoops low to take notice of all his people, in all their stations, all through history. What kind of condescension is it to be the lofty one who takes on human flesh and dwells among people on earth, to even die for them, to bring them the truth, to save them, to give them gifts, and yet find they still sin against him? What act of condescension is greater than Christ's?[32] To sin, then, against such knowledge, such infinite loftiness, such infinite condescension of Christ, is to sin against the very mercy of God.[33]

Mercy is hardly felt by hardened sinners. Edmund Calamy said, "Covenant-breakers are reckoned among the number of those that have the mark of

---

[31] Edwards, Jonathan, *The Works of Jonathan Edwards*, Volume 4, (New York, NY: Leavitt and Allen, 1852) 180.
[32] "And no man hath ascended up to heaven, but he that came down from heaven, even the Son of man which is in heaven," (John 3:13).
[33] "For I came down from heaven, not to do mine own will, but the will of him that sent me," (John 6:38).

reprobation on them."[34] Does this mean a covenant breaker cannot be pulled back into the fold? No, they can, by the power of the Spirit. The reason Calamy said that is because, that is not the way Christians act.[35] They do not act like Manasseh. They have been given the Spirit of Life, the Spirit of holiness, and the Word to guide them if they would simply listen.

There is hope in Christ to overcome sin, for he is the Living Word who directs you, reader, out of sin; he always gives you a way out. But one cannot trample the Son of God under his feet and walk away with continued sin and think God will turn his ever-watchful eye away. He is all seeing. He sees you every time you sin. You think to yourself, "When I was in secret and I," yes, he saw you. "When I was thinking the other day and"...yes. "When I was"...yes. He knows you will sin before you do and gives you a way out of it through the knowledge of the Word (1 Corinthians 10:13). Do you take it? Do you want to take it? Will you continue sinning or not? Will you continue to use the weakness of your sinful

---

[34] McMahon, C. Matthew, Editor, *The Covenanted Reformation*, <u>A Sermon at London by Rev. Edmund Calamy</u>, (Coconut Creek, FL: Puritan Publications, 2009) 335.

[35] "Seeing then that all these things shall be dissolved, what manner of persons ought ye to be in all holy conversation and godliness," (2 Peter 3:11).

disposition as an excuse? Is it simply better to ask for forgiveness than permission? Does Jesus allow men to make excuses in this way? Will Christ dismiss it as nothing? Manasseh is remembered for being the most wicked king. Here in 2 Chronicles 33 it is recorded. He is the *most evil*, worse than the heathen nations. How will *you* be remembered in God's book?

It is a sad state to continually sin against mercy by sinning against the work of the Spirit; this is the unpardonable sin. It is to attribute the work of the Holy Spirit to the devil. Is this not what people do when they reject God's law, making it beneath them, or something they snub at? One cannot sin against the work of the Spirit in this way. Several passages of Scripture speak of a sin that cannot be forgiven, after which a change of heart is impossible. Scripture even says that at that point, it is not necessary to pray for such people. It is generally known as the sin or blasphemy against the Holy Spirit. Jesus speaks of it explicitly in Matt. 12:31-32. This sin is impenitence persisted in to the very end, and declining the work of grace, rejecting it as if it was of the devil himself. All the prompting and prodding and wooing of the Spirit is rejected. All the ministers, all the preaching, all the warning, is rejected. Louis Berkhof said, "the sin consists in the conscious, malicious, and willful rejection and slandering, against evidence and conviction, of the testimony of the Holy Spirit respecting the grace of God in Christ, attributing it out of hatred and enmity to the prince of darkness. It is nothing less than a decided slandering of the Holy Spirit, an audacious declaration that the Holy Spirit is the spirit of the abyss, that the truth is the lie, and that Christ is Satan."[36] Did Manasseh sin in this way? Some people think to themselves, "I have often sinned against knowledge and conscience, and I fear I have committed that unpardonable sin, the sin against the Holy Spirit, and so I do not dare apply Christ's blood to myself." Though the sin against the Holy Spirit is a sin against knowledge and conscience, yet every sin (every grievous sin) against knowledge and conscience, is not the sin against the Holy Spirit. Such sins against the Word, those sins a Christian sins, are without malice in the heart, which this unpardonable sin cannot be. So, though you might often sin against knowledge and conscience, yet if you have not sinned with a malicious heart, *i.e.* you have not sinned merely because you want

---

[36] Berkhof, Louis, *Systematic Theology*, (Biblical Training, electronic edition).

to displease God, and grieve his Spirit purposefully, derailing his grace as the work of the devil, you have not committed the sin against the Holy Spirit. However, consider the following.

Sinning against the knowledge of God is sinning against Christ's mercy to you. It is not a matter of committing sin, it is a matter of stopping it. All Christians sin, and they sin in ways that are great and in ways that are little. All sin is accounted as sinning against God's mercy no matter its size. It is sinning against the Christ. And to sin against the Christ, is to sin against the very person and act of infinite mercy. You will sin as a Christian; you will not be perfect. The question, practically, is not to downplay it, into some Pharisaical comparison of the "I'm not nearly as bad as Manasseh is, so I have nothing to worry about." You have the Bible. You have more divine light than Manasseh had even with God sending prophets to him. The Bible is filled with warning passages that only those who are enlightened with the Spirit of God can understand, and those warning passages are there for you.

I taught a Sunday School class where one student said, upon reaching Hebrews 6 about trampling the Son of God underfoot, "That passage doesn't apply to me because I'm elect." This is horribly a wrong understanding of what it means to be a covenanted believer, much less being one of God's elect. If you dismiss God's warnings, if you reject the messengers he sends to you in that way, you are already on the path of Manasseh; *that is what he did.* He rejected the word, God's ministers, directives, statues and laws, all God's warnings. That Sunday School student was, in fact, doing exactly what Manasseh did with God's prophet – they were thinking, "those Bible verses, God's message there, that doesn't apply to me." O! contraire, *yes, it does.*

The aggravation of sinning against God's holy word, against knowledge, lies chiefly in that the more knowledge you have, the more God's will is revealed to you and the greater degree there is of it in guilt.[37] As you grow, you learn more; growing is commanded. You know things now, that even sometimes, you wish you didn't because hard theological ideas often cause trouble in the Christian life with other people not as blessed to see or understand it. Knowing those things makes church life more difficult. It makes the Christian walk harder. It requires more of you. It makes your Christian walk more exclusive. So, you must be aware that sinning

---

[37] "Therefore ye shall receive the greater damnation," (Matt. 23:14).

against what you know to be true makes sin all the more heinous in God's sight.

This has a special application to sins of the heart, your most beloved sins. Beloved sins? Yes, besetting sins, presumptuous sins; sins you won't give up yet and keep them close to your heart because you love them. Manasseh had many that he cultivated constantly. Whatever it is, whatever your sin is that you wrestle against and deal with day after day that has yet to be mortified and killed, every time it is committed, and you know you shouldn't do it, you sin against knowledge. "He has shown you, O man, what is good; And what does the LORD require of you But to do justly, To love mercy, And to walk humbly with your God?" (Mic. 6:8). But, sin makes us all stupid. Whether big or small, sin causes you to reject the word, sin against knowledge and give way to your passions. In every sin, you, in a practical manner, despise the mercy of Christ.

When sins occur and reoccurs this way, when it is not checked, or not mortified, the Apostle Paul warns that it will sear the conscience (1 Tim. 4:2). People who continue in these acts are given over to them. "Ephraim is joined to idols, let him alone," (Hos. 4:17). Jesus said of the blind leading the blind, "Let them alone," (Matt.

15:14). Don't give them any more knowledge. Don't warn them. Don't snatch them from the fire. Leave them be. Let them cook in their sin and against his mercy; let them ripen for hell, let them alone. What a horrible thought that sins lead people into places where even God says "enough is enough!"

Like Manasseh, we have the word, but we have more of it. We have more of the word, and the fullness of Christ. What will we do with it? What will we do with our service to him knowing that sinning against the knowledge of God is sinning against his mercy?

Chapter 3: Manasseh's Humiliation and Restoration

"Wherefore the LORD brought upon them the captains of the host of the king of Assyria, which took Manasseh among the thorns, and bound him with fetters, and carried him to Babylon. And when he was in affliction, he besought the LORD his God, and humbled himself greatly before the God of his fathers, And prayed unto him: and he was intreated of him, and heard his supplication, and brought him again to Jerusalem into his kingdom. Then Manasseh knew that the LORD he was God," (2 Chron. 33:11-13).

In 2 Chron. 33:11-13, we find God's judgment on Manasseh's wickedness. Because of Manasseh's wicked and evil works, because he was acting and living like an incarnate devil, God brings his promised calamity through divine judgment. There is some added information in this narrative in 2 Kings 21 and 24. "Moreover Manasseh shed innocent blood very much, till he had filled Jerusalem from one end to another; beside his sin wherewith he made Judah to sin, in doing that which was evil in the sight of the LORD," (2 Kings 21:16). These acts were demonic, wicked, evil acts of bloodshed. The bloodshed alone filled Jerusalem from one end to the other; this is hyperbole to some extent, but at the same time, quite horrific in its description. "Surely at the commandment of the LORD came this upon Judah, to remove them out of his sight, for the sins of Manasseh, according to all that he did; And also for the innocent blood that he shed: for he filled Jerusalem with innocent blood; which the LORD would not pardon," (2 Kings 24:3-4). He as an idolater of the worst sort; he had other men's sin on his account for seducing them, and causing them to err, and he was known as a *murderous butcher.* He even sacrificed, not only his children, but lined the streets red with blood of the innocents of others. He was, for all intents and purposes, in league with the devil carrying out the will of his father. He was pulling sin, as with a cart rope as Isaiah says, "Woe to those who draw iniquity with cords of vanity, and sin as if with a cart rope," (Isa. 5:18). Because Manasseh king of Judah has done these abominations, *something ethically disgusting,* (he has acted more wickedly than all the Amorites who were before him, and has also made Judah sin with his idols), "therefore thus says the LORD God of Israel: 'Behold, I am bringing such calamity upon Jerusalem and Judah, that whoever hears of it, both his ears will tingle. And I will stretch over Jerusalem the measuring line of Samaria and the plummet of the house of Ahab; I will wipe Jerusalem as one wipes a dish, wiping it and turning it upside down. So I will forsake the remnant of My inheritance and deliver them into the hand of their enemies; and they shall become victims of plunder to all their enemies, because they have done evil in My sight, and have provoked Me to anger since the day their fathers came out of Egypt, even to this day,'" (2 Kings 21:11-15).

"Wherefore the LORD brought upon them the captains of the host of the king of Assyria, which took Manasseh among the thorns, and bound him with fetters, and carried him to Babylon," (2 Chron. 33:11). The thorns are hooks in the nose; with chains around him leading him to captivity. God's toleration of Manasseh ended and he brought in the Assyrian army to overthrow the wicked King. Even source documents from Assyria mention Manasseh twice under Esar-Hadden and his successor Ashur-banipal. This captivity is specifically tied to the reality of rejecting the knowledge of God when that knowledge came to him by

Chapter 3: Manasseh's Humiliation and Restoration

God's ministers; he didn't listen. As a side note, God sends his ministers to bring light to the people, and when they reject it, God sees that as rejecting him. So, because of his sin, and because he did not heed the ministers God sent him, he was taken.

These captains "took him among the thorns, and bound him with double chains of brass, and brought him to Babylon." They took him with hooks. The hook or ring which was drawn through the gills of large fish when taken is what this refers to, (*cf.* Job 40:26), and is synonymous with a ring[1] which was passed through the noses of wild beasts to subdue and lead them. The expression here is both literal and figurative in some respects; a play on words. Manasseh is seen as an abominable beast, which the Assyrian generals took and subdued by a ring in the nose. The figurative expression is explained by the next clause: they bound him with double chains. נְחֻשְׁתַּיִם are double fetters of brass, with which the feet of prisoners were bound (2 Sam. 3:34; Judges 16:21; 2 Chron. 36:6, *etc.*). But they made him walk – the phrase "carried him to Babylon" is that he was taken away in a most horrible manner. If one was objectively looking at this man in the day this man lived,

---

[1] 2 Kings 19:28; Ezek. 19:4.

one might think that being carried away with a hook in the nose, and with chains, is a light punishment for his crimes. He killed his children. He caused all manner of wickedness of every abominable kind. Why would God only take him away in a forced humiliation for such acts? The reason is based on God's saving providence.

Verses 12-13, "And when he was in affliction, he besought the LORD his God, and humbled himself greatly before the God of his fathers, and prayed unto him: and he was intreated of him, and heard his supplication, and brought him again to Jerusalem into his kingdom. Then Manasseh knew that the LORD he was God," (2 Chron. 33:12-13).

Bitter affliction was Manasseh's portion. God brought him very low comparable to the height he was at. In contrast to his self-willed fame, he is now in the dungeons of Babylon. What does one do in prison? He thinks, he ponders his ways, he ponders what he had done for decades. The children he burned in the hands of Molech. The murders he committed in the city of Jerusalem, so well-known that they reached from one end of the city to the other. The blood in the streets. The pouring of blood in the streets. The dripping of blood in the streets. The smell of blood in the streets. The visits

Chapter 3: Manasseh's Humiliation and Restoration

and entreaties with demonic sources, the witches, the sorcerers, and the like. What would have been going on in his head? What would he have considered in this? Decades of will-worship, Satanic worship, evil doing, got him no further than a stinking dungeon. That's what will-worship does – it does not enhance the spiritual journey but detracts from it. It is ruinous. Could it be that in thinking about all this, he was reminded of his father Hezekiah, and about real religious piety? Hezekiah's prayerfulness? God's blessing Hezekiah prolonging his life? God's blessing in Hezekiah's faithfulness...in his reforms of worship?

Then, after some undisclosed amount of time, something very strange, very unconventional occurred – Manasseh implored the Lord his God – Yahweh Elohim. This "imploring" is a state of being grieved or weakened to dismay. It is to be as sorry as one can be in great sadness; to be utterly humiliated to physical sickness. As when someone says, "I made myself sick over it." One simply has to put themselves in the shoes of Manasseh for only a moment and consider all the aborted children that he killed and cause Judah to kill. "What have I done?" What prodigal manner would this be in being so taken back at his evil works? He did not entreat the idols. He has no idols around him. How does one entreat an idol in a dungeon, in a foreign country? He would no longer entreat of the gods he *made*, for now he owned the one true God as his God. God *alone*, with no other rival.

    Manasseh humbled himself greatly before the God of his fathers. He brought himself into humble subjection to God. It says he did this with *much force*. And he appealed to the God of his fathers, the covenantally faithful God, whom he knew he was not faithful to. What word, what message rang in his ears? What commandment, what warning? It does not say what he might have remembered, or what he might have pondered. But he does make a covenant renewal. Now he pondered and heard the Word of God. Now he was not rejecting it. Now he was remembering it. He entreats God in great force while under immense affliction. And so, Manasseh prayed to the Lord. The Hebrew idea is that he entreated God to intervene. "If My people who are called by My name will humble themselves, and pray and seek My face, and turn from their wicked ways, then I will hear from heaven, and will forgive their sin and heal their land," (2 Chron. 7:14). Manasseh was contrite and poor in spirit, subjected himself in humility and prayed. He knew that verse; he would have heard it at some point in the Scriptures. Manasseh was bound in a prison, but no sooner did he humble himself, pray and repent, that God made him free. He did not immediately walk out of the prison, but if the Son sets you free, you will be free indeed.

Verse 13b, "...and [God] heard his supplication, and brought him again to Jerusalem into his kingdom. Then Manasseh knew that the LORD he was God," (2 Chron. 33:13). God heard him. God's promise is that he hears those who in sincerity repent and turn to him. Manasseh repented. Manasseh turned back in humility. Manasseh was brought low; this humility is the same as repentance. As a result, God brought him back to Jerusalem. The details on that are not given, nor are they important. The text focuses on Manasseh being reformed and converted.

What does it mean that Manasseh "knew the Lord was God?" This was a fruit of his conversion, not the cause. This is seen as divine illumination. He did not see this, and now he did see this. He did not know it, for decades, but now he knew it. When one has new life in them, they see life quite differently; perspectives change. Did the Law and the Statues and the Judgments previously recorded that Manasseh had access to in the Word say Yahweh was Lord God Almighty? Of course they did. They said a great many things that were not new to him. Why did he believe now? Manasseh was now illuminated to its truth in God's providence by the Holy Spirit. He knew it by experience in himself. He knew it by the Holy Spirit in him. The Spirit illuminated his mind to the truth. Then? and not before? Joseph Hall said this, "Could his younger years escape the knowledge of God's miraculous deliverance of Jerusalem from the Assyrians? Could he but know the slaughter that God's angel made in one night of a hundred fourscore and five thousand? Could he but have heard the just revenge upon Sennacherib? Could he be ignorant of his father's supernatural recovery? Could he but see that everlasting monument of the noted degrees in the dial of Ahaz? Could he avoid the sense of those fifteen years which were superadded to his father's age? What one of these proofs does not demonstrate that God is the Lord? Yet, until his own affliction and cure occurred, Manasseh knew not that the Lord was God."[2] Sometimes it takes the rod to learn the truth. It would

---

[2] Hall, Joseph, *The Works of Joseph Hall*, Volume 2, (Oxford: Oxford University Press, 1863) 212.

have been much better, comparatively, for Manasseh to have experienced the sweet mercy of God in some kind of spiritual prosperity and peace while he was king, or on his ascension to the throne. But if he must be taught by the rod of God's judgment for his conversion, it is no less for God's glory. He sinned against knowledge before, and now, as a result of his conversion, he embraces knowledge whole heartedly.[3] The truth was the truth no matter what, no matter where it would lead him.

Consider in all this that humiliation precedes conversion. First, when the Lord sends knowledge, and it is to be believed, Christians find that it first humbles men before a change can take place in the mind. Humiliation is not a bare act. It is not self-appointed, or self-generated. It contains in it being of a contrite and poor spirit, but it is not something the self can generate apart from grace. It is based on the Word of God understood and exercised in grace. It is as the Apostle Paul calls such sorrow, "Godly sorrow," (2 Cor. 7:10). It derives from the Holy Spirit and his fruit in the soul. It is the beginning of conversion and part of regeneration.

---

[3] "I hate vain thoughts: but thy law do I love," (Psa. 119:113). "Great peace have they which love thy law," (Psa. 119:165).

Second, the quality of humility that God accepts comes from supernatural grace. The knowledge of one's self and sinful misery, without the knowledge of God and his supernatural mercy and grace, would be troubling. The sickness would be known without the medicine. "I'm evil and I'm going to hell, but I have no remedy. What is the knowledge and power of salvation in God's Word that directs me to walk, talk, live in the right way?" Humility is a jewel set in the Christian's helmet of salvation which relies on God's grace for its effectiveness.[4] It directs the sinner to honor God and his glory which is due to him.[5] Consider, that it debases the sinner so that God will pay attention to him. "God resists the proud, but gives grace to the humble," (James 4:6). God does not pay attention to those who are proud. Pride is opposite. It causes the sinner to desire God's crown, to place it upon his own head. Did not Manasseh do this originally? Stephen Charnock said, "But saving knowledge sinks man to the dust without sinking him to hell; lays him flat on the earth, thereby to raise him to heaven. For true knowledge, and a melting heart, are

---

[4] "Humble yourselves in the sight of the Lord, and he shall lift you up," (James 4:10).
[5] "For God resisteth the proud, and giveth grace to the humble," (1 Peter 5:5).

inseparable companions."⁶ Manasseh's knowledge of God was useless without the frame of humility to set it in. This is why Christ was so adamant, "Without me you can do nothing." Knowledge is not salvation, though salvation cannot be had or exercised in true faith without it. Such a humility is a grace that comes from God. "That He [*God*] might humble you," (Deut. 8:16). "LORD, You have heard the desire of the humble; You will prepare their heart," (Psa. 10:17). "My God will humble me among you," (2 Cor. 12:21). It is a spirit of conviction wrapped in a sight of sin motioned by the Spirit of Grace. It is the work, in this way, of the Spirit of God. There is no godly sorrow apart from the work of the Holy Spirit. "He will convict the world of sin, and of righteousness, and of judgment," (John 16:8).

The Spirit's conviction precedes repentance. This is called Evangelical humiliation – a term used by the Reformers and Puritans often. Manasseh was stricken by the law of God, his statues, judgments and commands which he previously broke; but now he sees the Word of God for its truth and goodness. If it were that he simply saw the law and understood it as it is

---

⁶ Charnock, Stephen, *The Complete Works of Stephen Charnock*, Volume 4, (Edinburgh: James Nicol, 1865) 52.

stated, we would call that legal humiliation. Esau sought the blessing with tears, but was not converted. Jonathan Edwards said, "Evangelical humiliation is a sense which a Christian has of his own utter insufficiency, despicableness, and odiousness, with an answerable frame of heart."[7] When Edwards says *frame of heart* he is referring to the supernatural grace of humility out of a changed heart.[8] It is a professed dependence on God through the work of Christ alone.[9]

Third, humility then becomes a container that receives the knowledge of God as both true and good. It enables the Christian to hold the Word not only as true, but also as morally good. Demons know the Word of God is true. But they do not experience it as good. God grants the sinner a gracious disposition where divine truth is successfully entertained in the mind and cherished in the heart. When someone is meek or humble in this way he welcomes truth and regards God's

---

[7] Edwards, Jonathan, *Religious Affections*, (Worcester, MA: Henry Plantiga, 1851) electronic edition, part 3 §6.

[8] "Not by works of righteousness which we have done, but according to his mercy he saved us, by the washing of regeneration, and renewing of the Holy Ghost," (Titus 3:5).

[9] "We also joy in God through our Lord Jesus Christ, by whom we have now received the atonement," (Rom. 5:11). "Neither is there salvation in any other: for there is none other name under heaven given among men, whereby we must be saved," (Acts 4:12).

truth as infinitely precious. He knows its origin – from God through Christ. He knows its power – in the Holy Spirit. He knows its purpose – a contrite disposition of heart. He knows its outcome –repentance to godliness. A humble soul desires to hold steadfastly to God's directions, and statues and laws and judgments, where the proud see God's Word as a yoke of bondage, as Manasseh originally did. Jeremiah 13:15, "Hear ye, give ear, be not proud." God's moral law is abused constantly by professing Christians in that way. They will acquiesce of its truth without knowing anything of its power and goodness.

Fourthly, humility is to be sought in light of God's statues, commands and judgments; in light of his word. "Seek righteousness, seek humility" (Zeph. 2:3). Where does one find what is right, or find humility? "Therefore, as the elect of God, holy and beloved, put on tender mercies, kindness, humility, meekness, longsuffering," (Col. 3:12). Where is instruction in this? "be clothed with humility," for "God resists the proud, But gives grace to the humble. Therefore humble yourselves under the mighty hand of God, that He may exalt you in due time," (1 Peter 5:5-6). "The LORD lifts up the humble;" (Psa. 147:6). *Humble* towards what?

Humility, but in what sense? "But to this man will I look, even to him that is poor and of a contrite spirit, and trembleth at my word," (Isa. 66:2). The word, the message, the good news takes center stage; and one must believe it.

Humiliation precedes conversion in the process of coming to faith.[10] God will humble sinners before he completely reforms them. I have never heard of a proud sinner converted while a proud sinner. There is no Scripture for that. *Pride cometh before the fall*, not before conversion. "And He received his entreaty, heard his supplication, and brought him back to Jerusalem into his kingdom. Then Manasseh knew that the LORD was God." Manasseh's disposition of humility preceded his prayer.

Reformation will only take place by God's method and power. This is only accomplished in humility. Humility is a fruit of the Spirit. It is a combination of meekness and gentleness, founded on great faith. Galatians 5:22-23 attributes this *only* to the Holy Spirit. It does not matter whether in the Old Testament or the New Testament. It is the same Spirit,

---

[10] See my work in the book *John 3:16*, where I discuss at length the exegetical aspects of the first 10 verses of being born again, which precede conversion, and how regeneration comes first.

same fruit, same humility cultivated by God in his people as a result of the substance of the covenant of grace applied to their soul. The penalties for disobedience for God's people in Leviticus refer to this explicitly, "And if by these things you are not reformed by Me, but walk contrary to Me, then I also will walk contrary to you, and I will punish you yet seven times for your sins," (Lev. 26:23-24). The absence of humility enacts judgment, not reformation.

God will reform them, meaning he will induce or cause them to abandon their evil ways.[11] It is a moral transformation, which is why we call being reformed, being *converted*. Reformation is just a biblical nickname for being radically changed by the Spirit. There is no sanctified reform, no conversion without being humbled by God first. No mortification of sin. No further sanctification of life. No growth in the Lord Jesus. No walking in the Spirit. No exercising one's self in the light.

God will add to knowledge the ability to process that knowledge by regeneration, by being born again.[12]

---

[11] "I will put my law in their inward parts, and write it in their hearts; and will be their God, and they shall be my people," (Jer. 31:33).

[12] See John 3:1-10.

What does it matter if a person has knowledge in their head that never translates down into the humility of their heart? If a person desires to be reformed, changed, then humiliation must occur first. The heart must be changed by God so that the knowledge becomes sanctified and the sinner's affections follow suit.[13] Without this humility, conversion will never occur. Without this humility holiness will never occur. God affects that change by making a new vessel from a broken one. God affects that by sending his Holy Spirit to enact the fruits of the Spirit in the life of the believer because belief in this way is humbling.[14]

Humiliation precedes conversion in two ways. First, in internal affliction through the power of Jesus Christ. It is an issue of the heart. "And I will give them one heart, and I will put a new spirit within you; and I will take the stony heart out of their flesh, and will give them an heart of flesh," (Ezek. 11:19). Christ is the great heart doctor that performs spiritual surgery on the

---

[13] "And I will give them one heart, and I will put a new spirit within you; and I will take the stony heart out of their flesh, and will give them an heart of flesh," (Ezek 11:19).
[14] "But the fruit of the Spirit is love, joy, peace, longsuffering, gentleness, goodness, faith, Meekness, temperance: against such there is no law," (Gal. 5:22-23).

sinner by the Spirit of Grace. He sends the Spirit to circumcise the foreskins of their heart, and change them. He gives them the ability to love Him as he loves them. It is a change explained by Christ in John 3. This is to be "born from above." God explains this time and time again all through the Old Testament. It is the heart of stone changed into the heart of flesh. "And I will give them a heart to know Me, for I am the LORD; and they will be My people, and I will be their God, for they will return to Me with their whole heart," (Jer. 24:7). We also find this all throughout the New Testament. For example, "For this is the covenant that I will make with the house of Israel after those days, saith the Lord; I will put my laws into their mind, and write them in their hearts: and I will be to them a God, and they shall be to me a people," (Heb. 8:10). "Forasmuch as ye are manifestly declared to be the epistle of Christ ministered by us, written not with ink, but with the Spirit of the living God; not in tables of stone, but in fleshy tables of the heart," (2 Cor. 3:3).

Second, in some cases external affliction accompanies it through the providence of God. These ways are not infallible, as if salvation in such ways always occurs. When bad things happen to people that does not mean God is always working salvation. Nor when good things happen that does not always mean God's blessings. Providence must be discerned. But if God so deems it necessary, afflictions can be used towards a happy end. God brought Manasseh low. Manasseh acted like a mentally affected rabid dog, so God had him publicly walked out of his kingdom with a leash through his nose bound in chains. It is no wonder that Manasseh didn't think out loud, "why has God not put me down, as a dog. Why have I not been sent to hell to burn for all eternity?" I would imagine such thoughts as these entertained him in his cell. Such afflictions for this man were necessary to his salvation. There have been many people throughout history who were wickedly sinful, and some tragic event, some afflicting providence befell them that Christ used to save them.

Maybe a disease, some malady, a war, intense riches with the greatest depression, extreme poverty, the extreme death of loved ones or families, or a host of other afflicting providences, not excluding the devilish work of a self-willed sinner in opposition to the Word of God. God alone orders all these things. He has his *Pharaoh's* and he has his *Manasseh's*. Pharaoh was hardened and lost. Manasseh was hardened and then softened. "Who maketh thee to differ?" The clarity of the humiliation preceding conversion is of great importance in the way professing Christians see salvation. How might this be applied to you and I?

Many have been humbled, or are even now being humbled in afflictions, but consider, that these may be a means to a further happy work. Edmund Calamy says, "For God so sweetens the bitter cup of affliction, that a child of God many times tastes more of God's love in one month's affliction than in many years of prosperity."[15] This is very true. Afflictions teach us in humility to know God experimentally and affectionately.[16] This is what we do in running to him, loving him, bowing at his feet in respect of his glory and sovereignty and looking to him to be our hiding place. It is what occurs when we cast all our cares on him for he cares for us. Some may say, but in those situations, I am not as humble as I ought to be. The degree of humiliation is not necessarily the issue. To one degree or another humility might be exercised in affliction – but what counts is the presence of the fruit of the Spirit in gentleness, meekness and

---

[15] Calamy, Edmund, *The Godly Man's Ark*, Sermon 1, (Coconut Creek, FL: Puritan Publications, 2012) electronic edition.
[16] "Behold, we count them happy which endure. Ye have heard of the patience of Job, and have seen the end of the Lord; that the Lord is very pitiful, and of tender mercy," (James 5:11).

humility before God. How do you know whether you have it or not? Consider it first in your conversion, not simply in your affliction.

Humiliation is an evidence of sincerity in your conversion. You might say, "I don't think I've ever been humbled for my sin." If that is the case, you have never been converted, which in turn makes all affliction that much more difficult. Maybe you were temporarily grieved over your sin – Esau was.[17] He even sought the blessing of God with tears. How have you wept for sin? Maybe you were disheartened by your sin – Judas was, he hung himself.[18] He was distraught, but without humility. Maybe you even had a worldly modesty like Pharaoh had when he wanted some kind of instant gratification from Moses that his affliction would cease. It was a worldly appeal to God of some kind. It was a

---

[17] "For ye know how that afterward, when he would have inherited the blessing, he was rejected: for he found no place of repentance, though he sought it carefully with tears," (Heb. 12:17).

[18] "Then Judas, which had betrayed him, when he saw that he was condemned, repented himself, and brought again the thirty pieces of silver to the chief priests and elders, Saying, I have sinned in that I have betrayed the innocent blood. And they said, What is that to us? see thou to that. And he cast down the pieces of silver in the temple, and departed, and went and hanged himself," (Matt. 27:3-5).

bargain – do this for me and I'll go to church. Do this for me and I'll let Israel go.[19]

You might even be soaked with false humility. False humility keeps Christ at arm's length. You don't want to do too much for God. You simply do enough to satisfy yourself. The "worm theology" that Christians have, you despise that. You don't like the idea of being debased, or don't want to hear too much of that. Like Pliable in *Pilgrim's Progress* wanted to hear of the good things, not the bad things of their journey; and when he met the slough of despond, he did not continue. False humility causes you to think you greatly love Christ, when really, you don't love him at all. You think far more of yourself than you do of God, and you will have none of that Christian duty. You want Christ *your way,* but not on his terms.

Consider, that I've been talking about Manasseh as the most wicked man of his day, but if you have false humility, you are among the worst of your day. Why? Because you sin against Christ the Messiah fully revealed, fully come, now in heaven, fulfilling all the

---

[19] "Then Pharaoh called for Moses and Aaron in haste; and he said, I have sinned against the LORD your God, and against you. Now therefore forgive, I pray thee, my sin only this once, and intreat the LORD your God, that he may take away from me this death only," (Exod. 10:16-17).

work which God covenantally had given him. He has fully come, fully demonstrated in power, and is fully exalted at the right hand of God. And yet, you sin against knowledge – the most knowledge that anyone has ever had of God's saving mercy in the history of the world. "The depth of hell calls to us for answerable humiliation; he that will not be humbled for his sins here, will be humbled and tumbled to the depths of hell hereafter," Henry Greenwood said.[20]

If you lack humility, can you get it? It's available only through Jesus Christ.[21] A humble sincerity is seen in a broken spirit before the Lord Jesus Christ. Again, a verse you should memorize, "But on this one will I look: On him who is poor and of a contrite spirit, And who trembles at My word," (Isa. 66:2). God pays attention to those he has enabled with a broken spirit to be poor and contrite, and to love his word. Is that your spirit? Would you classify your spirit as humble, contrite, and poor? It is a false humility that *hopes* they are lowly and contrite. Or is it a real humility worked by the power of the Spirit, day by day?

---

[20] Greenwood, Henry, *Tormenting Tophet*, (Coconut Creek, FL: Puritan Publications, 2013) electronic edition, part 3.
[21] "By the which will we are sanctified through the offering of the body of Jesus Christ once for all," (Heb. 10:10).

Chapter 3: Manasseh's Humiliation and Restoration

    A humble sincerity is seen in a complete and utter dependence on the work of God. It changes "I did" to "Christ did it through me." Jesus says, without me you can do *nothing*. Is that your dependence? Manasseh was weak and sick in mind and heart. In such a prayer and supplication, he entreated God in lowliness. Prayer should be sincere, reverent, humble, importunate, submissive and filled with faith. This was Manasseh's prayer. Did God hear? Yes. Did God hear right away? Yes. Did God act right away? The text is *silent*. The prison doors certainly didn't magically open up for him. How long was he entreating? How long after God heard him did he take him back to Jerusalem? What would that day have been like when the jailor came down to release him from the jail cell and tell him that he was going back to Jerusalem? Would it have been a wonderous thing to him? Would he consider it an answer to prayer? Would it have even humbled him more thinking about what he was going back to? What were the people doing? What would they think of him? What would he need to do to really repent? Would he fall back into his old sins? Would he give the nod to others in their sins which he started? Would the streets run red with blood again?

A humble sincerity is a total surrender to the Word of God no matter where it takes you. The Word, the Christ, the Logos, the eternal Word of God is your all. You can't part with him, and you cannot part with his Word which directs you, sustains you, guides you, gives you your marching orders for King Jesus as a faithful solider. That you will be able to say, "I know the Lord, he is God." Manasseh said that, according to the text, upon his arrival into Jerusalem. He was outspoken about it. Someone had to know because he was outward about it. The Chronicler had to hear it from him in some way. A consideration of all those providences he faced mixed together and summarized in a single praise. "I know..."

Apply this all, then, to your affliction and humility. A broken spirit is the disposition that Christ looks for in you.[22] Your utter dependency is what he looks for.[23] Your total surrender is what he is after in you. Crying out to Christ is an act of faith in Christ's power to save. When Manasseh cried to the Lord out of the prison, and repented of his former sins, and, because

---

[22] "Blessed are they that mourn: for they shall be comforted," (Matt. 5:4).
[23] "I am the vine, ye are the branches: He that abideth in me, and I in him, the same bringeth forth much fruit: for without me ye can do *nothing*," (John 15:5).

he believed in the promises of God, and His word, and the coming of the Messiah, the Lord heard and granted him mercy. What *great* sins he did. But, was there a greater sin in Peter's denial of Christ three times? (Matt. 26:7). Yet, he repented, and he was forgiven. What about all those who crucified the Christ? Have there ever been greater sinners than these men, who with their wicked hands crucified the Lord of glory as the Apostle says? (Luke 22:53 and Acts 2). They were, afterwards, while Peter preached, pricked in their consciences, and Peter tells them to repent, and they did, and they found mercy. You see that sinners are worse in some ways than others are, but there is salvation to be had and it all begins with humility before God. "Come now, and let us reason together, saith the LORD: though your sins be as scarlet, they shall be as white as snow; though they be red like crimson, they shall be as wool." (Isa. 1:18), and you should think that this is only accomplished through God's Anointed Savior.

I end this chapter with this warning: what a terrible thing it is for people in the church today to come just so far in religion, but without humility.[24] They came only so far, but not all the way. To them they are

---

[24] "*Almost* thou persuadest me to be a Christian," (Acts 26:28).

Christians, but they were not part of God's eternal kingdom in Christ, participating in all the benefits of the Son or receptive to Christ's salvation in godly humility. They only came so far, but not as far as wicked Manasseh in humility. They might be very upstanding Christians from all worldly perspectives. Good in church, prayer, devotions, leading the family, reading their Bible as occasion warrants. But are they false? Manasseh was a devilish, wicked, monstrous butcher, killer, sinner, Satanist, name him what you will. I believe he is one of those fellows in the text of the Bible that give despondent people hope because even with a murderous wretch like Manasseh, for God rescued him. *Manassehs* can be rescued.

    There are no excuses to not be rescued if such a one as Manasseh, as Adam, as Paul can be transformed. God will grant humility to those who ask for it. But be reminded that such is a difficult position and prayer to require at God's hands. For Manasseh, it required hooks and chains and dungeons and exile. I'd imagine that his daily ration of food was not so good, and that his tattered clothes over time were quite miserable. His cell mates were the rats and the refuse. For some the obtaining of humility by the Spirit of Grace may have joined to it many trials. But as much as humility brings us low, it is also like an elevator where we must ride up to the roof to see Christ's throne at the top. Pride casts us down, and humility must raise us up.

If you are humble, the grace of God belongs to you. "He resists the proud and gives grace to the humble." Learn humility of God, who humbled himself from heaven to earth, to exalt you from earth to heaven, to such a glorious kingdom (where the proud shall not enter and be shut out) the Lord Jesus brings us for his mercy's sake! *Manassehs* are only rescued by Jesus Christ if the fruit of humility seasons the work of prayer, repentance and faith, because, humiliation always precedes conversion.

Chapter 4: Manasseh's Reformation

"His prayer also, and how God was intreated of him, and all his sin, and his trespass, and the places wherein he built high places, and set up groves and graven images, before he was humbled: behold, they are written among the sayings of the seers," (2 Chron. 33:19).

Take a moment to read the entire passage of 2 Chronicles 33:14-25.

The monstrous, abominable, repulsive, offensive, provoking sins of Manasseh and the people he seduced to do evil are recorded in 2 Chronicles 33:1-10. Manasseh was the most wicked man of his day, not only in his own right, but also in the seduction of the people to follow the wickedness of his sins. His sins were in fact his life, and they especially revolved around anti-biblical worship. He did not worship God in truth, nor by the prescription set down by God. In contrast, he made a league with the devil and instituted witchcraft, consulted mediums and sorcerers, engaged in human sacrifice, and committed all manner of heinous sin, which was so bad that he was known as a murderous butcher from one end of the city of Jerusalem to the other. The Chronicler writes in this way, specifically, to make the reader disgusted by all his actions.

These sins went on for decades; it was not a week, or month, or even a year. It was for the better portion of his life. Imagine the hardness of his heart? In all this wickedness, God had decreed a specific point of toleration where he set it to a bar and said, "it will only be to here and no more." He sent prophets, seers, messages, the Word of God to Manasseh, and he did not listen to God; and he did not let the people listen to God. It doesn't say they didn't listen to the prophets, but, that in God's ministers bringing the Word to the people, they did not listen to God. God's voice is heard speaking in the mouths of his ministers. At this time of cut off, at this specific bar of sin, God then had the armies of the Assyrians capture Manasseh, lead him off with hooks through his nose like a junkyard dog and marched him in his chains of brass and chains of sin to Babylon to be thrown into the dungeon, and imprisoned.

In prison, in that dank, dark place, Manasseh repented. God converted this abominable sinner, and in humility (*repentance*), he prayed, sought God, and God listened to his entreaty and supplication. God brought him back to Jerusalem, answered his prayer, and the text says that Manasseh "knew the Lord he was God." No longer was he sinning against knowledge. Now he fully and without reservation embraced the God of his fathers.

When Manasseh got back to Jerusalem, what did he do? Imagine walking the streets, seeing the people, seeing the places of worship defiled. Imagine seeing the temple with his own idol in it. The Chronicler gives a sense of urgency in the text. Verse 14, "After this he built a wall outside the City of David on the west side of Gihon, in the valley, as far as the entrance of the Fish Gate; and it enclosed Ophel, and he raised it to a very great height. Then he put military captains in all the fortified cities of Judah." Before, in all manner of sin, he opened Jerusalem to the sins of the nations. Now he constructs barriers to the nations and closes them off. Protection, border walls, were built all around the city. Manasseh was not politically pressing a need but took the country by storm and immediately fortified the walls of Jerusalem. This was his first act after his conversion with the people. Why? It was fortified physically. It was a further strengthening of the wall Hezekiah his father had started.

It was also fortified spiritually. Get inside Manasseh's head for a moment. He looked to delete the triggers that spring up and cultivate besetting sin through temptation.[1] He looked to rid the country of the open tendencies they had to foreign power, foreign religion, and close up the city, the church, the people by even working the angle of out of sight, and out of mind. Verses 15-16, "He took away the foreign gods and the idol from the house of the LORD, and all the altars that he had built in the mount of the house of the LORD and in Jerusalem; and he cast them out of the city. He also repaired the altar of the LORD, sacrificed peace offerings and thank offerings on it, and commanded Judah to serve the LORD God of Israel."

Reformation, as it always is with everyone who engages in it, was immediate for Manasseh, and yet extensive to a great degree. He took away all the foreign gods. He took away the idol he had made in the house of the Lord. He took away the altars and cast them out of the city. He repaired that which was in disrepair for God's worship. He then instituted peace offerings and thank offerings. He reinstated right worship. "Besides

---

[1] "Blessed is the man that endureth temptation: for when he is tried, he shall receive the crown of life, which the Lord hath promised to them that love him," (James 1:12).

the cakes, as his offering he shall offer leavened bread with the sacrifice of thanksgiving of his peace offering," (Lev. 7:13). Why? "It is most holy," (Lev. 7:1). He instituted again, the most holy acts of corporate worship. He submitted himself before the Word of God. He removed things that hindered true worship. What would the people think at this point? *Who is this? Is this not Manasseh?* I'm sure some of them did not engage in such reformation as they should have. *Wasn't this that same Manasseh who seduced us to do evil?* Now, he commanded Judah; not seduced Judah, commanded, to serve only the God of Israel. The Hebrew thought here is to work or serve God alone as God so prescribed. But even though he did this, there was still a problem.

Verse 17, "Nevertheless [*what a terrible word in the text*] the people still sacrificed on the high places, but only to the LORD their God." There is a word, it is an ancient Hebrew word, in the oldest manuscripts and oldest Arabic writings encapsulating this idea with *a use of force*. It is the word "nevertheless." It can literally mean "of a truth, or truly." It can also have connotations of the idea of "no, but instead this..." It may more definitely be translated "howbeit". *Nevertheless,* they still did what they should not have done. *Nevertheless,* they did not hearken as they should have. *Nevertheless*, they should have done "A" but instead continued in their sin to do "B." Even though Manasseh began a hearty reformation of religion, nevertheless, the people did not completely stop their idolatry; they did not comply. They sacrificed to the Lord their God, but, they couldn't give up the pomp and circumstance of idolatrous worship. What would Manasseh have been thinking here? Would he have been reminded of his own rebellion? Would he have cried and wept and thought about all the times he didn't listen? Would he have some measure of mercy to the people? The *Regulative Principle*[2] of God's worship was being enacted by penitent Manasseh, and the people just wouldn't follow suit. God alone determined, by his word, the manner in which these sinners should approach him in this time before the coming of the Messiah. But, the half-hearted attempt of their reform just could not overthrow their

---

[2] Referring to Psalm 115:4 and 135:15, Calvin wrote, "Whence had idols their origin, but from the will of man?" "It is, moreover, to be observed, that by the mode of expression which is employed, every form of superstition is denounced. Being works of men, they have no authority from God (Isa. 2:8,13; 7:57; Hos. 14:4; Mic. 5:13); and therefore it must be regarded as a fixed principle, that all modes of worship devised by men are detestable." (*Institutes of the Christian Religion*, 1:11:4).

habit. They were given over to a sinful addiction that would not be so easily broken.

"Now the rest of the acts of Manasseh, his prayer to his God, and the words of the seers who spoke to him in the name of the LORD God of Israel, indeed they are written in the book of the kings of Israel. Also, his prayer and how God received his entreaty, and all his sin and trespass, and the sites where he built high places and set up wooden images and carved images, before he was humbled, indeed they are written among the sayings of Hozai. So Manasseh rested with his fathers, and they buried him in his own house," (2 Chron. 33:18-20). It is three times mentioned, (2 Chron. 33:13, 18, 19). Consider the word order of these three acts. Here is the way these verse lay out the process: prayer, supplication, prayer, God received it, prayer again, humility, lowliness, then he was *humbled.* Manasseh's conversion was accomplished by the Word of God, by the Word of the seers. Is this not an interesting note? 2 Chron. 33:18, "and the words of the seers who spoke to him in the name of the LORD God of Israel." God's ministers preached to him, and something got through. The Spirit used something God said through them to change him. And he in turn looked to change the worship of God back to

Chapter 4: Manasseh's Reformation

what God had prescribed for the good of his people. Things that would point back to the anointed coming of the Messiah, instead of away from him.

"Then his son Amon reigned in his place. Amon was twenty-two years old when he became king, and he reigned two years in Jerusalem. But he did evil in the sight of the LORD, as his father Manasseh had done; for Amon sacrificed to all the carved images which his father Manasseh had made, and served them. And he did not humble himself before the LORD, as his father Manasseh had humbled himself; but Amon trespassed more and more. Then his servants conspired against him, and killed him in his own house. But the people of the land executed all those who had conspired against King Amon. Then the people of the land made his son Josiah king in his place," (2 Chron. 33:20b-25). Those closest to the king, those under his immediate signs of humility, repentance, and reformation, would not allow the church to go back into idolatry and so they took it upon themselves to kill this new king. They lifted their hand civilly and unjustly before God. They struck down the Lord's anointed. As a result of this conspiracy, they were killed by the people justly, for murder against the Lord's Anointed.

Manasseh and Amon could not have been more different, and yet, more alike. One would have hoped in seeing Amon following suit in reformation. But from his very name, Amon, named after an Egyptian god, his downfall is Chronicled in contrast and similarity to Manasseh. They were both kings, and idolaters and they both suffered.

Manasseh was taken by the Assyrians; Amon was conspired against and killed by his own servants. But they differed in significant ways. Names. Manasseh was named after a tribe of the Israelites. Amon was named after an Egyptian god. Their length of reign. Manasseh ruled Judah for fifty-five years Amon for two years. God determines the bounds of their habitations and the length of their days. Their spiritual revival. Manasseh repented, turned to God, and lived, reviving true religion and worship. Amon died as an idolater and hardened sinner, and revived idolatry in the end. Manasseh died a natural death. Amon died a violent and tragic death. "Then the people of the land made his son Josiah king in his place,"

The account of Amon's reign is the shortest in Chronicles. It acts almost as a short appendix to his father's reign. Amon undoes the reformation of

Manasseh, and the mission of his son Josiah will take that up in a very thorough reformation later. Nothing more is known about the conspiracy of verse 24, and nothing certain about the people of the land in verse 25. This book, does, however, end this section with a note of hope. We find under Josiah the most thorough and happy reformation of all the kings.

Believers are to be striving against the sins they once loved while at enmity with God; and that with great resolve.[3] Spiritual life enlivens the sinner to now be "up and doing" in rightly discharging his duties before God in striving against sin. The Reformers and Puritans used a phrase throughout their exhortations to Christians in the discharge of their duties before God. "In the fear of God, then let all of us be *up and doing*, doing what we may for the furtherance of this great work of reformation," John Brinsley (1600–1665).[4] "Be *up and doing*. The journey to heaven is a long and difficult way; and to fit yourself for heaven is a great work," Francis Roberts (1609-1675).[5] "The Sun of

---

[3] "Ye have not yet resisted unto blood, striving against sin," (Heb. 12:4).
[4] Brinsley, John, *Stand Still*, (Coconut Creek, FL: Puritan Publications, 2013) 108.
[5] Roberts, Francis, *The Natural Man directed to Jesus Christ*, (Crossville, TN: Puritan Publications, 2015) 86.

righteousness is up and shining, therefore we should be *up and doing*," Nathaniel Vincent (1639-1697).[6] "I call upon everyone that would be counted a friend of Zion, to be *up and doing*, to be much and active in pious and precious endeavors for the perfecting of Zion's deliverance, and the establishing of Jerusalem in peace and truth," Humphrey Hardwick (no dates).[7] Up and doing....what? Opinions vary. Circumstances vary. Historical contexts vary. The Christian church, as Christ's divine institution, takes the Word of God alone, and the whole Word of God, as her only rule of faith.[8] This is the faith once for all entrusted to the saints. This *up and doing* is tied to the divine directives of the word. The church must frame a statement of what she understands the Word of God to teach. They must know and apply what God says. The reason is that the church has various duties before God which must be accomplished, but cannot unless Christians know what those duties entail. Once Manasseh was enlivened to faith, he took God's Word and immediately

---

[6] Vincent, Nathaniel, *The Day of Grace*, (Coconut Creek, FL: Puritan Publications, 2012) 65.
[7] Hardwick, Humphry, *The Precious Seeds of Reformation*, (Crossville, TN: Puritan Publications, 2015) 108.
[8] "Ye should earnestly contend for the faith which was once delivered unto the saints," (Jude 1:3).

implemented reform. He was up and doing in contrast to being lazy and apathetic. His reforms first dealt with sin, based on the Word of God alone. Based on what he commanded the people to do. He took away triggers to sin, and patrolled the people by the city walls to make sure that what came into the city would not undo these reforms now being accomplished.

Spiritual life which causes men to be *up and doing* enlivens the understanding to God's will in striving against sin. That which God commands is always the Christian's duty. As Christians have opportunity to do their duty before God in every circumstance, they are to perform it. "So likewise ye, when ye shall have done all those things which are commanded you, say, We are unprofitable servants: we have done that which was our duty to do." (Luke 17:10). Tired, lazy, busy, are all excuses that slowly turn obedience to disobedience. But this is especially fueled by ignorance, or rebellion...as in Manasseh's case. Once converted, Manasseh is the opposite of being creative for the ways of wickedness, but rather, diligent in the work of reform. Christians should always be in a right state of mind and heart to do what is required as occasion offers.

And they are to be led by the Spirit into all good works no matter where the Word of God would take them.[9]

The aim of God's commandments is conformity to God's character, or Christ's holiness, in order for God to gain the most glory. "You shall be perfect", is Christ's directive to his ministers, his apostles, in Matthew 5-7 and the sermon on the mount, which emphasizes their zealous endeavor to be salt and light, mimicking the perfection of the Father.

Christ was always *up and doing* and spiritually empowers his people to be *up and doing*. The work of Christ and its subsequent blessing is a benefit to believers. They receive the whole spiritual blessing in him. The anointed Savior empowers them to be *up and doing* but doing *rightly*. They are to be imitators of God to render acceptable sacrifices, living sacrifices, holy and pleasing to God.[10] Such only occurs through the Lord Jesus Christ. Christ was about his Father's work from the get go. When he was only twelve, he was already in the temple teaching, being about his "Father's work."[11]

---

[9] "If we live in the Spirit, let us also walk in the Spirit," (Gal. 5:25).
[10] "I beseech you therefore, brethren, by the mercies of God, that ye present your bodies a living sacrifice, holy, acceptable unto God, which is your reasonable service," (Rom. 12:1).
[11] "And he said unto them, How is it that ye sought me? wist ye not that I must be about my Father's business?" (Luke 2:49).

After all his work was done and complete, after his death, resurrection, ascension, and exaltation, is he not the great High Priest enabling and empowering his mystical body through the Spirit of Christ, by way of his blessed intercession?[12] Christians and churches all over the world have no excuse to not be *up and doing*. What do they not have or need from Christ that causes them to be unfaithful? They only have the excuses they fabricate.[13] *Nevertheless...*

Spiritual life follows God's will to perfect holiness, not misplaced sincerity in striving against sin. When Christians sincerely break God's commandments, or sincerely do anything contrary to God's word, at no time does God excuse the sin because they are merely sincere. Manasseh was no doubt sincere in his attempt at revitalizing worship and holy living after his conversion. His reformation was built on "commanding" according to God's rules, not seducing according to his own self-will. God's Word implemented – to be *up and doing* what God says. This is the reason Christ's merit in upholding the law

---

[12] "Seeing then that we have a great high priest, that is passed into the heavens, Jesus the Son of God, let us hold fast our profession," (Heb. 4:14).
[13] "And they all with one consent began to make excuse," (Luke 14:18).

perfectly is imputed, or reckoned to the sinner's account, because sinners can't be perfectly sincere in their discharge of their duty in the way God requires. "Without me you can do nothing." Christ says. God accepts a believer's sincerity based on Christ's fulfillment for them. The spirit is indeed willing, but the flesh is weak. But that does not give the flesh the excuse to do nothing. It is true, "Joshua said to the people, "You cannot serve the LORD, for He is a holy God. He is a jealous God," (Josh. 24:19). *Ought* to be doing does not imply *can* be doing, or doing according to the desires of the heart. Yet, they *must* be up and doing. They must be up and doing rightly, and this can only occur by the power of the Spirit in them. Manasseh's change invoked a hearty sincerity to do what God desires, regardless of whether the people would follow him or not.

    Could you see them wondering what got into this man? Building a wall, taking out places of worship, destroying idols. Was there not a great amount of talk behind his back? Then, *nevertheless* – hear that awful word again; *nevertheless*, they rejected the right rule of execution. As much as Manasseh did in striving against sin, it was too little, too late. Sin ruined his whole life; and even though, upon his conversion, he was now *up and doing* everything in reverse, and reform, they, *nevertheless* were not so moved. When he repented, and demonstrated his hatred of what he had formerly done, God returned to him by great mercy. Nevertheless, the people had so degenerated into idolatrous worship that no matter what Manasseh commanded them, they still worshipped in the high places in the way they wanted, instead of the way God wanted. They were, for all intents and purposes, addicted to wickedness; they were addicted to what they loved. Every ancient commentator on this passage uses the same phrase – Manasseh's *half-hearted reformation*. Sincerity aside, Manasseh had so seduced and degenerated the people into wickedness that true worship which was now being re-introduced, was boring. They wanted the pomp and circumstance that was being ripped away from them. Take away our high places, our interpretive dance, our Ashtaroth poles, our special music, our spiritists, our organs, our witchcraft, our overthrow of prescribed worship. The people, for all intents and purposes, were doing some right things, but all of it in a wrong way. It is a sad thing when Christians do the right thing in a wrong way.

In this text, it confers to the reader the importance of godly worship and piety. Worship has a form and method. Even in the basics of the commandments, the first four tell Christians the object, means, the manner and the time for worship. It is what we call the first table of the law.

Christians often imagine a true objective with a false method. The Christian sometimes thinks, "so long as we come to worship the Living God, we can do anything we want in worship. If we honor Christ, if we honor God in what we do with sincerity, God will accept it." *No*, the Roman Catholic teaching that "whatever God does not forbid he allows" is false, and devastating to worship. It blemishes it all. It is unfortunate that so many churches in so many places all throughout history have never escaped the traditions of men. "In vain they worship Me, teaching as doctrines the commandments of men," (Matt. 15:9). It is a very sad thing when a minister says, "what you are suggesting that I do is to overthrow what the church has always been used to, and if I do, they will throw me out, and then, what shall I do to feed my family?" This kind of thing is happening all over the world today. They think, "A little reform is enough;" but remember, partial reformation is a *full offense to God*. Did God heartily bless all Manasseh's works? Was reform according to God instituted? Or was it relatively easy for Amon to implement those same sins his father had in his earlier years?

The right method of worship revolves around the *Regulative Principle*. God *alone* determines the manner in which sinners approach him. Chapter 21:1 in the *1647 Westminster Confession of Faith* says, "The light of nature showeth that there is a God, who hath lordship and sovereignty over all, is good, and doth good unto all, and is therefore to be feared, loved, praised, called upon, trusted in, and served, with all the heart, and with all the soul, and with all the might. But the acceptable way of worshiping the true God is instituted by himself, and so limited by his own revealed will, that he may not be worshiped according to the imaginations and devices of men, or the suggestions of Satan, under any visible representation, or any other way not prescribed in the Holy Scripture." Samuel Willard said, "Men go to the house of God, and attend on his worship in those ordinances which he has instituted, and they add to them a worship which he never gave any order about."¹⁴ It is that implementation of that horrible word: *nevertheless...*

Worship, or any duty, never takes place in biblical sincerity unless the method matches the command. At no time, can the right rule of executing biblical worship be rejected whether in the church or in the life of the Christian.

Be *up and doing*, but take a point from Manasseh in doing too little too late. It is no doubt honorable, and no doubt, godly for that man to have been converted, and then immediately to be *up and doing all he could*. Though Manasseh was up and doing, he would not do *everything* needful. That would be left to Josiah's very thorough reformation.¹⁵

When you are *up and doing* any spiritual duty before God, you cannot ever reject the right rule of execution even if you think you are sincere. Doesn't God accept your sincerity as a Christian as a duty? Not as a duty, but in the duty. The lack of power to do more in a duty does not destroy the acceptance of what is done from a willing Christian mind because God accepts his

---

[14] Willard, Samuel, *The Sinfulness of Worshipping God with Men's Institutions*, (Coconut Creek, FL: Puritan Publications, 2011) 29.
[15] 2 Chron. 34:1ff.

people's will for the duty accomplished, but only because of Christ. You do something pious. You do it sincerely. You do it rightly executed, such as hearing a sermon. You've prepared your heart. You've received a good night's sleep. You've thought about distractions and are working to keep yourself focused. You incline your ear to listen. You have your Bible ready and follow along in the text, *etc.* But if you were to ask yourself, "I've done this duty to hear the sermon in such a way as to do it *perfectly*," what Christian would ever answer *yes?* It may be a duty accomplished in the right way but lacking full power. That is far different than a duty done with sincerity to God but in a wrong method or manner not prescribed by God. God accepts his people's frailty because they are washed and plunged under the fountain of Christ's blood.[16] You bring Christ to hearing the word, and so God accepts that sacrifice as if Christ had done it. This is accepted by God as holy. It is the only way in which anything is received by God as an appropriate spiritual sacrifice.

God is not interested in consulting you on how you think he should be worshipped or obeyed.

---

[16] "And the blood of Jesus Christ his Son cleanseth us from all sin," (1 John 1:7).

Manasseh commanded the people to reform their worship, but they did not listen. He initially did not listen, but they would not listen. Their addiction to sin overthrew their ability to hear rightly. Do *you* listen? I hear it constantly by myriads of people, especially through my online work with *A Puritan's Mind*, "I just don't believe that," they say. Historical Theology, and the church at large believes it, but you don't? Really? The entire Christian church believes it, but you don't? Would it not at least be safe to say that you might be missing something important in your understanding if everyone else believes it and you don't? They won't take that time, because tradition or feeling is better suited to them; it's *easier*. Too many people will leave their church, too many people will make their life difficult, too many people are in disagreement with them. At the time, how many disagreed with Manasseh when he came back to the city? Did they all follow all his commands? As confessional Christians, I find them to be most odd in this way especially concerning worship. And was not worship Manasseh's main objective once he was converted? "I just don't believe worship should be done that way according to accepted Christian truth," someone thinks. It doesn't matter that every member of the Westminster Assembly believed it, or the confession says it, as if all of them were wrong, *and you're right*. Where did they get such odd ideas, I wonder, that you would reject it, and they all would accept it? Whenever the straight jacket of doctrinal truth is wrapped around them, they get uncomfortable because the Word of God says to them, *you can't be that way; and they simply don't like that*. "I don't accept those teachings as true." But, your sincerity in advocating false truths doesn't matter. And so there, they will have none of that kind of conversation. That's one of the great *advantages* about being *confessional*. Everyone in history advocating a confession together believed the same thing. Scripture exposited rightly leads everyone to the same fountain of life because God's foundation of truth never changes.[17] It makes no difference if you consult someone in the early church, or someone in the Old Testament, or someone in the New Testament, or someone in the middle ages, or someone from the Reformation or someone from the era of the Puritans, or the Princeton Theologians. Orthodox

---

[17] "But this man, because he continueth ever, hath an *unchangeable* priesthood. Wherefore he is able also to save them to the uttermost that come unto God by him, seeing he ever liveth to make intercession for them," (Heb. 7:24-25).

theology has a *consensus*. This is why the whole of Christian doctrine is called the *rule* of faith. If there is an argument or difference of opinion, the Bible wins, as it is exposited biblically transmitted in concise detail in the confession. It will always win in its *consensus*. There is no non-consensus on any important doctrinal point in the Christian faith, through the whole of historical truth. Truth does not evolve. It is merely discovered and preached more accurately. It is simply a matter of getting everyone on the same page through the guidance and leading of the Spirit of Truth through faithful teachers and ministers. This is what Manasseh attempted to do.

Your religious duty includes sincerity but it is not the deciding factor as to whether it is acceptable before God or not. Did God accept worship in the high places because the people worshipped the living God? No. Their sincere endeavor was voided by their sin. God was not there. God was not in it. God did not accept it. The men that offered sacrifices in the high places, they came to the temple too. God says, "I am Almighty God; walk before Me and be blameless," (Gen. 17:1). So, "that He might present her to Himself a glorious church, not having spot or wrinkle or any such thing, but that she should be holy and without blemish," (Eph. 5:27). And therefore, "worship the LORD in the beauty of holiness!" (Psa. 96:9).

You must be *up and doing* according to the Word. When you are up and doing in personal piety or religious worship of any kind, it must be according to God's method and manner. Jesus Christ was zealous for the institution of God's true worship in his house of prayer.[18] Christ will not have vain worship after the traditions of men. We do such and such because our church has always done that. We do such and such because its new and novel. We add this or that because it attracts people to the church. We do this because we believe it honors God and we are sincere when we do it. Christ will never tolerate anything but that which is in accordance with God's method and manner. Jesus began his public ministry by cleansing the temple. John 2:14-17, "And He found in the temple those who sold oxen and sheep and doves, and the moneychangers doing business. When He had made a whip of cords, He drove them all out of the temple, with the sheep and the oxen, and poured out the changers' money and overturned the tables. And He said to those who sold doves, "Take these

---

[18] "And his disciples remembered that it was written, The zeal of thine house hath eaten me up," (John 2:17).

things away! Do not make My Father's house a house of merchandise!" Then His disciples remembered that it was written, "Zeal for Your house has eaten Me up." The modern church would never have succumbed to this. They would have set up a booth next to the other vendors, become their friends, and would have attempted to win them to the "truth" over a course of time by identifying with them in their sincerity. Jesus drove these men out with a whip. Why the contrast? Christ had an unmitigated zeal for the truth of the Word and a desire to see true worship instituted (*cf.* John 4:24). It is worship *about him, to him* and he will never accept nor receive anything less than what he prescribes and desires. God *alone* determines the manner in which sinners approach him in every station of life.

Be up and doing quickly. In worship, in personal piety, in family worship, in Christian duties of all kinds, as you are up and doing, so you must be up and doing rightly and quickly. Manasseh ran out of time; this was a factor for his reform failing. Can you imagine him walking the streets on his return, having repented and been saved, and yet seeing his handiwork from one end of the city to the other? What would he start to do? How could he fix things, and what would he begin with? The wall; was it so important? It was – it was a means of physical and spiritual protection from sin. It was also an object lesson for us to rid ourselves of all triggers that might cause us to not be up and doing. Christians who have gambling problems don't walk through casinos to test the viability of their constitution. Christians who were addicted to alcohol don't go to bars. Triggers are eliminated. Walls are erected.

Life is short[19] in accomplishing what these duties are to accomplish in the glorification of Christ and the sanctification of the believer. Either you are *up and doing*, or you are part of the *nevertheless* crowd. God gives us no middle ground.

Manasseh immediately implemented what was right, but he was just not thorough enough, nor did he get to the people soon enough. His own son was an evil wicked king. His people were still stained with innocent blood, and worshipped in high places. They were not going to be so easily persuaded to cast off their sins. They were not humbled together. They just listened to the *commands* of the newly reformed king. Josiah, in differentiation, caused them to come together and stand

---

[19] "For what is your life? It is even a vapour, that appeareth for a little time, and then vanisheth away," (James 4:14).

in the covenant reading the book of the law to them. We do not hear of the Word attached to the commands of Manasseh as it was with Josiah. No covenant. No reading of the word. No causing them to understand it.

The time of *up and doing* is now. Some people are blessed to be born into covenant homes.[20] Some people are saved later in life. Some are early, some are later. God has never called all his elect at once, but some come to him sooner, and some come to him later. Andrew and Peter were first called. Then Philip. Some like Timothy are called and set apart at an early age, some come to be converted later. Lydia and the jailer were converted in what, middle age, (Acts 16)? Manasseh about sixty years of age, near on his death, (2 Chron. 33:19), Josiah, as a youth. But God gives everyone one life to be *up and doing* to strive against sin and to be holy. All have one life to live in repentance and godly humility before God. All have one life to please king Jesus. All have one life, whether they die at 12, 20 or 120. All have exactly the right amount of time for their life, for their duty, for their work before God. Be up and doing, according to the word, and with all speed, that you may take advantage

---

[20] "And that from a child thou hast known the holy scriptures, which are able to make thee wise unto salvation through faith which is in Christ Jesus," (2 Tim. 3:15).

of the time you have in order to please Christ with as much zeal and truth as you possible can before you die. Please him in holiness, for holiness leads to happiness, and this is all wrapped up in the duty of being up and doing before God in striving against all sin and conforming to the image of Christ.[21]

---

[21] "Conformed to the image of his Son," (Rom. 8:29).

Study Questions

I don't want to merely give you a concluding remark as an ending to this work. Instead, I want to give you an opportunity to consider what was said by way of *remembrance*. Often, we read a book, and it goes back onto the shelf. We forget about it, and it renders us little spiritual benefits except what we might have gleaned here or there in our *speedy reading*. Instead, use the following sections below to consider how the life of Manasseh may be beneficial to you spiritually. It may be that you are unconverted and need Christ, and you think that God couldn't possibly forgive you because you think your sins are bigger than Christ is a Savior. Or it may be that you are converted and you wonder daily how God puts up with such a wretch as you might think you are, which in turn is robbing you of assurance in Christ.

Take some time in your personal devotions to consider the following questions:

CHAPTER 1: MANASSEH'S WICKEDNESS

Study Questions

1. Manasseh is said to be a wicked wretch from the time he started reigning on the throne. He grew up in a covenant home. Did you? How did being trained up in a covenant home affect your life for the better or for the worse? If you didn't grow up in a covenant home, what would you have missed out on? Why would growing up in a covenant home be helpful?
2. "Train up a child in the way he should go: and when he is old, he will not depart from it," (Prov. 22:6). What does this verse mean?
3. What is the Law of God?
4. Do people only do evil before they are converted? What does it mean to *do evil?* Can evil people do good things in God's eyes?
5. Of the lengthy list of Manasseh's recorded sins, think about what three you would place as the most wicked. Have you ever done those sins as blatantly as Manasseh did? Why or why not?
6. What does it mean to "provoke God to anger?" How would you describe what this means to a friend? How do you provoke God to anger?
7. What does it mean that God never changes? Is this a helpful thought to you, or a disturbing

thought? Is God's unchanging nature a comfort to you? Why or why not? How would you explain that God is without passions or parts?

8. What rule has God given his people that they might know how to please him in all things?

9. What is idolatry? What is self-love? How do they complement one another? How are these sins present in your life?

10. Is there a rival in your own heart next to Jesus Christ? How can you overcome your besetting or presumptuous sins?

CHAPTER 2: MANASSEH'S WICKEDNESS PART 2

1. Why does God deal with people according to keeping the Law or not keeping it? How do blessings and curses work in keeping the Law or not? Do you keep the Law perfectly as God requires? What happens to those who do not keep God's Law perfectly? Who kept the Law perfectly for you?

2. Manasseh caused other people to be seduced to sin. Do you do that? Have you ever caused others to run into sin with you?

Study Questions

3. Why is sinning against God with knowledge worse than not having that knowledge?
4. What does it mean to be illuminated by God? Have you experienced this in your own life? How would you describe this to someone else?
5. How does God keep his promises? Are you a good promise keeper? Do you keep all your promises to God?
6. What did Manasseh do with his children? Why is this such a terrible sin?
7. Why must God punish all wickedness? How is sin punished through Christ?
8. What is ignorance? How can ignorance be alleviated in your own life?
9. When is mercy hardly felt by hardened sinners? Do you feel God's mercy? How do you know you have the mercy of Christ working in your life?
10. What does it mean to be forgiven by Christ?

CHAPTER 3: MANASSEH'S HUMILIATION & RESTORATION

1. Did God punish Manasseh? How did he do this? Did the punishment fit the crime? Why didn't

God kill Manasseh for his crimes? What did God do to Jesus Christ for the sins of Manasseh?

2. What does it mean for someone to be in bitter affliction?

3. How did God save Manasseh? How did Jesus Christ save Manasseh? How was Christ's grace applicable to Manasseh?

4. What does it mean that Manasseh was humbled? How is repentance seen as humbling? Have you ever repented? How would you describe your repentance to someone else? How would you define *repentance?*

5. Explain how humiliation precedes conversion. What is conversion? Are you converted, and how do you know?

6. What is *evangelical humiliation?*

7. What is the evidence of being converted in your own life, or in any believer's life?

8. How can understanding Manasseh's conversion aid in giving you a greater assurance of salvation?

9. What is the role of the Spirit's work in converting people?

10. How does God's providence sometimes work out in afflicting a soul for their conversion? Do

Study Questions

you know anyone like this? Has this happened to you? What would you say to someone "in the dungeon" who is entreating God about what Christ can and will do for someone if they sincerely repent?

CHAPTER 4: MANASSEH'S REFORMATION

1. What was the significance of Manasseh building the wall as the first listed accomplishment after his conversion? Why was it physically and spiritually important?
2. Why is reformation always immediate after someone is truly converted? Did this happen to you? How did you "reform" in your life?
3. What is the Regulative Principle of Worship? Why is it important today as much as in Manasseh's day?
4. What happened with Manasseh's son Amon, and how is he characterized differently than Manasseh, or similarly to him?
5. What does it mean to strive against sin? Do you do this? How?

6. What does it mean to be "up and doing"? How does this work out in your life before Christ's watchful eye?

7. What does it mean to be "up and doing" according to the Word? How is the Word of God tied to "doing" anything before God?

8. What does it mean to be conformed to God's character? What role does the Law play in this?

9. What is godly worship and piety? How would you describe someone who engages in godly worship? What would someone's personal devotions look like that engaged in godly piety?

10. If someone is sincere in what they do before God, is that all God desires? Does sincerity breed acceptability? Why or why not?

AFTERTHOUGHT:

1. How does studying Manasseh's life help you if you are not yet a convert to the Christian faith? What steps will you take to become a disciple of Jesus Christ?

Study Questions

2. How does studying Manasseh's life help you with furthering your assurance before God if you are sincerely converted by Jesus Christ? What steps will you take to cultivate a deeper faith, assurance and liveliness in your Christian walk?

Other Helpful Books by Puritan Publications

5 Marks of a Biblical Church by C. Matthew McMahon

5 Marks of a Biblical Disciple by C. Matthew McMahon

The Reformed Apprentice Volumes 1-4: Workbook on Reformed Theology, Hermeneutics, the Doctrine of God and Private Devotions by C. Matthew McMahon

Rules for Our Walking with God by Jeremiah Burroughs (1599-1646)

The Christian's Duty to Walk Wisely by Matthew Mead (1630-1699)

Walking Worthy of the Gospel by Nathaniel Vincent (1639-1697)

Directions for Daily Holy Living by Daniel Burgess (1645-1713)

The Zealous Christian by Simeon Ashe (d. 1662)

www.ingramcontent.com/pod-product-compliance
Lightning Source LLC
Chambersburg PA
CBHW022110090426
42743CB00008B/792